I0145449

A Noteworthy Americans
Quick Reader Biography Book

Sky Rider

The Story of Evelyn Sharp,
World War II WASP

by Jean A. Lukesh

Field Mouse
PRODUCTIONS
Grand Island/Palmer, NE

Text copyright © 2011 Jean A. Lukesh - Cover © 2011 by Ronald E. Lukesh
Published by Field Mouse Productions
Grand Island and Palmer, Nebraska
All rights reserved
First Printed in the United States of America, December 2011
Photos: Courtesy of Thomas and Eric Palmer and
Mary E. Farmer Palmer Collection, Irene Auble Abernethy,
Diane Ruth Armour Bartels, or as otherwise cited in photo captions.
Maps, photo conversion, and cover ©2011 by Ron Lukesh.
Front Cover Photo: Evelyn Sharp climbing into a P-51
(*The Woman's Collection, Texas Woman's University, Denton, Texas*)
Back Cover Photo ©2011 by Ron Lukesh: Diane Ruth Armour Bartels, author of *Sharpie,* with Dr. Jean Lukesh, author of *Sky Rider*, at the WASP Memorial in the Veterans Memorial Garden in Antelope Park, Lincoln, Nebraska; with Evelyn Sharp's flag and Congressional Gold Medal (not shown).
A Noteworthy Americans Quick Reader Biography
R.L.: 5.6   I.L.: grades 5 through adult
Cataloging-in-Publication Data
Lukesh, Jean A., 1950—
Sky Rider: The Story of Evelyn Sharp, World War II WASP
SUMMARY: A young adult quick reader biography of Evelyn Sharp, an adopted girl who overcame asthma and many other problems and learned to fly an airplane as a teenager. She became the youngest woman commercial pilot, taught men to fly for war, and was a respected member of such women's flying groups as the WAFS and WASP. Until her early death in an airplane accident in 1944, she flew warplanes across America and Canada so that men could fly them into battle during World War II—and left a legacy that helped open the way for the women pilots of today and tomorrow. (Includes vocabulary/glossary, index, select bibliographies, and critical thinking pages.)
This Noteworthy Americans Quick Reader Biography is
Suggested for ages 11 to 112
1. Sharp, Evelyn Genevieve, 1919-1944—Biography—Juvenile.   2. Nebraskans—Biography. 3. Women air pilots. 4. Aeronautics. 5. World War II—Women—Biography.   6. Adopted Children.   7. Air pilots.   8. Women Airforce Service Pilots (WASP). 9. Women's Auxiliary Ferrying Squadron (WAFS). 10. Women in the military
Title. II. Subtitle.   III. Series.   B [920] [978.2] [973.91] [629.13] [355]
ISBN 978-0-9647586-3-6

Note: Terms written in Bold type that are not chapter headings or section headings are vocabulary glossary terms.

Dedicated to:

Dr. Glen Auble who always championed Evelyn Sharp.
His daughter Irene (Auble) Abernethy who let me
borrow the Auble family scrapbooks, photos, and stories.
My father-in-law, Emanuel "Gabe" Lukesh,
who knew and flew with Evelyn and told us about her.
Diane Ruth Armour Bartels, who wrote THE ultimate
biography of Sharpie and who worked with us.
Thomas and Eric Palmer (Evelyn's second cousins),
who let us use the late Mary Farmer Palmer Collection.
Dean Misko for remembering Evelyn and Gabe.
The people of Ord who keep Evelyn's memory alive.
The Ninety-Nines (99s) for their soaring efforts, and
The Women pilots (WAFS and WASP), who flew
so men pilots could fight in World War II.
Texas Woman's University for housing WASP archives.
Other WASP archive sources for their help.
The men and women of the U.S. Armed Forces,
past and present, who protect and defend us,
And all veterans, families, and citizens who support them.
Today's pilots and others who dare to reach for the sky.
And all those who dream and work
to make a positive difference in life.
We thank and salute you!
Also to all the Lukesh great-grandchildren: Logan,
Sylvie, Haley, Cole, Emmalea, Madaleine, Ian, and Noah,
and also to Britnee, McKenzee, and Colby,
who are all free to be who they want to be.
As always, to Ron who keeps me on task,
to Bo Dog, who used to guard my feet as I wrote,
and to Jasper who is learning to be our new guard dog.

Time Line for Evelyn Sharp

1919   October 1 or 20, Evelyn born in Montana, is soon adopted

1922? Sharp family moves to Hastings, Nebraska, later to Erickson

1930? Sharp family moves to Ord; Great Depression has just begun

1935   February 4, first flight lesson

1936   March 4, Evelyn solos

1936   November, Evelyn earns her private pilot's license

1937   January, Evelyn joins first new Nebraska chapter of the 99s

1937   May, Evelyn graduates from high school

1937   July 2, Evelyn's woman pilot hero Amelia Earhart is lost at sea

1937   August, Business people in Ord help Evelyn buy a plane

1937   September, Evelyn is 1st pilot to land at Arrasmith Field

1938   January, Evelyn has to give up Taylor Cub; Ord holds benefit
       dance for her to go to Lincoln Airplane and Flying School

1938   April/May, Evelyn makes Theater and Air Mail appearances

1938   May, Evelyn attends Lincoln Airplane and Flying School; earns
       Transport (Commercial) License; CPTP starts in December 1938

1939   July, meets "Aunt Elsie"

1940   June, Evelyn becomes a CPTP pilot, teaching others to fly

1941   December 7, WWII starts

1942   January, Evelyn does not join Cochran's women pilots program

1942   October, Joins Nancy Love's WAFS program, as an "Original"

1942   November, "Aunt Elsie" visits Evelyn on base

1943   January, Evelyn visits Elsie and learns the truth about her mom

1943   March, friend Cornelia Fort dies in crash

1943   June, Evelyn is 1 of first 4 WAFS qualified to ferry the P-51

1943   August 5, WASP formed; Evelyn to command at Palm Springs

1943   September, *Ladies Courageous* movie stars on base

1943   December, Evelyn is 1 of only 2 women in 200 pilots to ferry
       pursuit planes to bases in mass ferrying effort

1944   March, Evelyn starts to qualify in B-17 and P-38

1944   March 30, Evelyn leaves on 1st leg of 5 day P-38 flight

1944   April 3, Evelyn dies in P-38 crash; April 9, Evelyn buried in Ord
       cemetery; December 20, WASP program is disbanded

1945   World War II ends

1948   Ord Air Field is renamed Evelyn Sharp Field

1977   Congress grants veteran benefits to former WASP members

1992   Evelyn Sharp is inducted into Nebraska Aviation Hall of Fame

1996   Diane Ruth Armour Bartels writes *Sharpie: The Life Story of
       Evelyn Sharp, Nebraska's Aviatrix*

2010   19 Nebraska WASP inducted, Nebraska Aviation Hall of Fame

2010   WASP receive Congressional Gold Medal at the U.S. Capitol

Table of Contents

Evelyn Sharp, about 6 years old, in a tire tube swing, at Hastings, Nebraska, 1925, around the time she first started dreaming about "driving" an airplane, a dream that would last a lifetime (Mary Farmer Palmer Collection, Courtesy Palmer Family)

Chapter 1:

To Drive an Airplane

Long ago, a little girl stood on a hill and looked up to the sky. There she saw a new kind of machine for the 1920s—an **aeroplane**, or airplane.

That little girl knew what it was, but she stood watching in wonder. Then she turned to her father and said, "Daddy, someday I want to drive an airplane."

That was the first of many goals she set—and achieved—for herself.

The little girl's name was Evelyn Sharp, and she would get her wish. She would overcome many problems and become one of America's youngest pilots—while still in her teens.

Her hometown in Nebraska even helped her buy her own small airplane. With that plane and others—and with her dog as her favorite co-pilot—she took more than 5,000 **passengers** for rides across the sky.

After that, she taught hundreds of men to fly for the coming war. Soon she became one of the first women in history—and one of the youngest—to be invited to fly for America's new **Army Air Forces** in World War II.

As a member of the **Women's Auxiliary Ferrying Squadron** (or **WAFS**) and then the **Women Airforce Service Pilots** (or **WASP**), she flew warplanes to Army air bases all across America and Canada. In that way, she freed up men pilots to fly planes in **combat** across the ocean.

With nearly 4,000 total flying hours, she also helped set the standards for America's highest-rated women pilots. Despite her experience and great talent, she was killed while flying her favorite kind of warplane during World War II.

Some people knew her as "Sharpie" because of her last name and her remarkable flying skills. Others called her "Sky Rider" or "the best of the best."

This book tells the story of Evelyn Sharp, a young woman who dared to set and reach high flying goals in a man's world—and who inspired other women pilots of her day and the future.

Chapter 2:

Changing Names, Dates, and Parents

Evelyn Sharp's early life was full of changes!

She always believed her birth date was October 1, 1919. But official records say her birthday was really the 20th of October of that year.

Her name was not even Evelyn Genevieve Sharp when she was born in Melstone, Montana. Her name at birth was Lois Genevie Crouse.

Her birth parents were Orla Crouse and Elsie Haeske Crouse. They had not known each other very long when they decided to marry.

Orla was much younger than his wife. He worked as a delivery man for the railroad. Elsie sometimes worked in a store or as a waitress.

Elsie Haeske Crouse, Evelyn's birth mother, in 1910, about nine years before Evelyn's birth (Photo Courtesy of Diane Ruth Armour Bartels)

Breaking Up

Orla and Elsie did not have much money, and they were not happy together. They were not ready to be married or to raise a family—but they already had a baby on the way!

They decided to split up before the baby was born. But Elsie had nowhere to go, and her own large family could not help her.

Finally, she went to Miles City where Orla's father and his new wife and family lived. He was a doctor, and there Elsie had the baby.

Elsie hoped things would get better for herself and her child. But that did not work out.

She and Orla decided to get a divorce. They would go on with their own lives, away from each other. Orla did not even see his new daughter.

Elsie had very little education, no job, and no money. She was living with strangers. Before long, she knew that she and her child did not belong there.

She loved her daughter, but she knew she could not get a job and take care of the baby, too. She did not know what to do.

Elsie and her in-laws talked about putting the baby up for adoption. They all wanted the child to have a better life.

Elsie knew she had to give up her baby, but she did not want to give her to an **orphanage**!

She wanted a loving couple to adopt her child. But where could she find a good, happily married couple who wanted—and who would take good care of—her baby?

A New Life

Then, a lucky thing happened. When the baby was about a month old, some of the Crouses' family friends named John and Mary Sharp came for a visit.

The Sharps were happily married, but they were not able to have children of their own. They really wanted a child, and they fell in love with Elsie's baby right away. They wanted to adopt her.

Everyone knew that the Sharps would be good and loving parents. So with tears in her eyes, Elsie agreed to give her baby to them.

John and Mary then adopted the child. They changed her name to Evelyn Genevieve Sharp. They took her home to Kinsey, another town in Montana, where they lived.

Evelyn would not even learn that she was

adopted until many years later. By that time, she was already an adult and well on her way to making a name for herself.

Evelyn in her baby carriage in Montana (Mary Farmer Palmer Collection, Courtesy of Palmer Family)

Baby Evelyn and her adopted mother Mary
Sharp (Mary Farmer Palmer Collection,
Courtesy of Palmer Family)

Chapter 3

Moving Again

John and Mary Sharp worked for the railroad in Kinsey. There they ran a **boarding house** where people rented rooms. They also owned and ran a pool hall, a dance hall, and a store.

For a while, things went well for the Sharp family. Then one day, a fire tore through their buildings. They lost almost everything they owned.

John Sharp wanted to get a fresh start in a new town. He moved his family to Billings, Montana. There the Sharps ran a grocery store.

Evelyn was not yet two-years-old when her family moved to Billings. By then, she had already lived in four Montana towns—Melstone, Miles

City, Kinsey, and Billings. She would live in many more places during her short lifetime.

Three-year-old Evelyn on a tricycle at Hastings, Nebraska (Mary Farmer Palmer Collection, Courtesy of Palmer Family)

Moving to Hastings

When Evelyn was still very young, her family moved again. This time they moved to Hastings, Nebraska.

There John Sharp bought a big two-story

house at 233 West High Street (now 9th Street). At that time, the house stood on one of the highest hills in town. It was not far from Longfellow Elementary School where Evelyn later went to school.

John and his wife used the front part of their big house as a grocery store. The family lived in the back rooms. They also rented out their second floor rooms to Hastings College students.

"Sunshine Vitamins" and Friends

Around that time, Evelyn began to show signs of having some health problems. Some of those would trouble her off and on for her whole life.

As a baby, she had not gotten enough milk or "the sunshine vitamins and minerals"—vitamin D and calcium. As she grew, her body did not have what it needed to make her bones strong.

That led to **rickets**, a painful bone problem. Getting the right vitamins and minerals and playing outside with friends helped her grow stronger.

Evelyn also suffered from **asthma**. That sometimes made it hard for her to catch her breath. One day, an asthma attack nearly killed her. That was a very scary time.

She would have other asthma attacks over the years. Still, nothing would keep Evelyn down for long. She was a happy, active, **athletic** child with many friends. She would be like that all her life.

Evelyn (center) with some of her many Hastings friends (Mary Farmer Palmer Collection, Courtesy of Palmer Family)

Chapter 4

Dreams of Flying

The Sharp family lived in Hastings for six or seven years in the 1920s. From her hill, Evelyn often watched airplanes fly over the town.

When she was five or six, she pointed to one of those planes and told her daddy she wanted to "drive an airplane" someday. Those words later became her lifelong dream and her first goal.

Different-Looking Planes

Those early airplanes of the 1920s and 1930s looked very different from most airplanes today. They all had **propellers**. They often had two or three rows of wings.

Most of those early planes were made of

wood and canvas. They were small, lightweight, slow, and not very powerful. They had few instruments and no radios.

A Man's Job

People in those days often said that pilots flew "by the seat of their pants." That means pilots flew by feeling the movement of the plane and reacting to it. It took a lot of both luck and skill to fly an airplane in those days.

Most pilots of that time were men. Many of them had just come back from flying missions in Europe during World War I. Airplanes were still a new tool of war and peace.

Flying was a man's job in those days. People thought flying was too dangerous for women to do. Then some women pilots, such as Amelia Earhart of Kansas, showed that they had flying skills, too.

Barnstormers

Many of those early pilots flew around the country. They stopped at towns to try to earn money with their planes. They showed off their flying skills at county fairs and other events. They also gave sky rides for a little bit of money.

In those days, there were very few airports, but that was not a problem. Pilots could land their small planes on almost any flat ground—even farm fields or roads, and sometimes frozen rivers—though that was very dangerous.

People often called those pilots **"barnstormers"** because they flew very close to the ground and just over the tops of trees and barns. They flew tricky turns and twists and loops in the air. Flying like that was not only dangerous. Sometimes it was deadly.

Flying Circuses

Some pilots in those days even flew with animals—to get people's attention. Down South, a pilot named Roscoe Turner flew with a lion cub in the backseat of his plane. However, the cub soon grew too big and had to be **grounded**.

Perhaps because of such animals in planes or because of all the action and activity, people called air shows **"flying circuses"** and were often fascinated by them

Hastings was a great place for Evelyn and others to see such airplane shows in the 1920s.

Whenever she could, little Evelyn watched the skies and dreamed of flying a plane someday. She would get her chance, as a teenager.

Evelyn with a doll, about the time her family moved from Hastings to the ranch at Ericson, Nebraska (Mary Farmer Palmer Collection, Courtesy of Palmer Family)

Moving to the Country

When she was about nine, Evelyn and her family moved away from her hill house in Hastings. They moved more than a hundred miles north to a ranch near Ericson, Nebraska.

Evelyn missed her friends, but she enjoyed living in the country. She helped her family grow garden crops. They sold those at the farmers' markets in town.

Evelyn really liked the animals on the ranch, too, especially the horses. She loved riding her own horse to Dry Cedar Country School on the Wheeler and Garfield county line. Evelyn was small, and her horse was tall—but that was no problem for an athletic girl like her.

The Sharps lived on that ranch for about a year. Then, a bad winter and money problems forced them to sell almost everything on the place, except Evelyn's horse Chalky.

When they moved again, the horse went with them.

Chapter 5

A Penny a Pound

In 1930, John Sharp moved his family about 25 miles southwest of Ericson to the town of Ord, Nebraska. That would be their last move for a long time.

The Sharp family moved into a house at 1634 M Street in the center of Ord. At first, John fixed lawn mowers to make a living, and his wife Mary ran a laundry.

Then they opened a café at their home. Soon they added a soda fountain, a candy kitchen, and a tobacco counter. Later John opened a bar on the edge of town.

Evelyn went to the city schools. She was a

good student, and she made friends easily. She was also a very good **athlete**.

Evelyn, age 11, her first year in Ord, 1930 (Mary Farmer Palmer Collection, Courtesy of Palmer Family)

Evelyn had her horse Chalky. Some of her friends had horses, too. They often rode around town, out into the country, or down to the river.

She loved dogs, too, so she often took her latest dog along wherever she went. That made living in Ord even more fun.

Still, Evelyn would not forget about flying. Many other people in Ord were very curious and interested in airplanes, too.

In October of 1930, an air rodeo or air show brought several planes and pilots to an airfield five miles northwest of town. (Airports were often called airfields then because most runways were made of grass or dirt.)

At that air rodeo, people could take a plane ride for just "a penny a pound" or whatever money the rider could pay. It was an exciting time, especially for airplane lovers like Evelyn!

Some of Evelyn's teachers even used that interest in airplanes to have their students design paper airplanes and lay out a pretend airport.

A few years later, Evelyn went to a real airplane school. There she learned to take real planes apart and put them back together.

Chapter 6

Horses, Dogs, and 5¢ Ice Cream

Living in Ord was like having the best of both town life and country life at the same time!

Evelyn really enjoyed doing things with her friends, but she had to work, too. The Sharp family never had much money, so John, Mary, and Evelyn all had to work hard to help pay bills.

In the 1930s, almost no one had money. That dry and windy time was often called the "**Dirty Thirties.**" It was also called the **Great Depression**.

Crops did not grow well in that dry time. People could not pay their bills. Many people lost their jobs and homes. Some banks even went out of business.

Evelyn was still a child, but she looked for ways to help her family. Whenever she could, she helped at home and with her father's businesses.

She worked hard and took her work seriously. But even then, she made work seem like fun.

She had a great sense of humor.

Evelyn, probably junior high age (Mary Farmer Palmer Collection, Courtesy of Palmer Family)

Ice Cream from a Horse Cart

One summer day, Evelyn came up with a fun way to help her family. Her father had rented an empty building downtown. He turned it into an ice cream factory. There he made ice cream that he sold in Ord and nearby towns.

Evelyn's dad had made a cart for her white horse Chalky. One day, Evelyn hitched up her horse. She loaded the cart with tubs of ice cream.

Then, she drove her horse and cart around town, selling the cold treats. She charged 5¢ for a double dip cone.

Evelyn and her dog standing next to the ice cream cart behind Chalky the horse. One of Evelyn's friends is inside the cart. Photo taken in Ord, Nebraska, 1932. (Photo Courtesy of Diane Ruth Armour Bartels)

When Evelyn was done selling ice cream, she unhitched the cart. Then, she and three of her friends climbed onto her big horse's long back. With her dog running alongside, they rode down to the river for a swim and a great time!

Learning To Give More

In the 1930s, very few people in America had jobs or money for ice cream or anything else.

People tried to get by, any way they could. In Ord, people did their best to help each other—especially their friends, family, and neighbors.

Those hard times even forced John Sharp to sell Chalky. Evelyn missed her old horse, but she knew she had to give up things to help her family.

In the years that followed, Evelyn and her friend Irene Whiting often borrowed horses from C.J. Mortensen, the banker in Ord. They rode everywhere together.

They also stayed very busy with school and community life, as well.

Chapter 7

The Best Girl Athlete in Town

In high school, Evelyn had plenty of activities to keep her busy. She took all the regular classes of the day. She also took vocal music, played in the band, and acted in plays.

Some school tests showed that she understood science and machines very well. That would help her a lot when she started flying later.

But Evelyn's favorite classes often involved sports of any kind. She took part in lots of athletics in school. She also played sports after school for two hours a night twice a week.

She played soccer, speedball, volleyball, basketball, and baseball. She enjoyed hiking, roller skating, bicycling, ice skating, golfing, tennis, swimming, and more.

In high school, she and one of her best friends were the only two girls to earn honors in sports all four years. By the time she graduated, her nickname was "the best girl athlete" in Ord—in school or out.

Evelyn taught hundreds of Ord children how to swim out at the river in the summer. (Mary Farmer Palmer Collection, Courtesy of Palmer Family)

All-American Girl

During the summer, Evelyn worked as a lifeguard. She taught swimming and water safety to hundreds of children. She did that at the river, because the town of Ord had no swimming pool.

In many ways, she was a real tomboy. She loved to be outdoors, hiking, riding horses, or doing other things. In the fall, she even liked to go pheasant hunting with the guys.

Evelyn and her high school friend Irene Whiting with horses they often borrowed from the banker in Ord. (Mary Farmer Palmer Collection, Courtesy of Palmer Family)

In many ways, Evelyn was like other teenage girls of the time. She was pretty and very popular.

She dated some of the boys in school and was friends with everyone. She loved to go to dances. She even made a lot of her own clothes.

Helping Others

Evelyn took part in many school, sports, and home activities. She also worked on church and community projects.

As a longtime member of Campfire Girls, she even taught some of the younger children. She became a role model for everyone.

When she was not doing other things, she worked for her parents. She worked to help her family pay their bills. All her life, she worked hard to help others.

One day, a man who lived at her family's boarding house had trouble paying his own bills. Her family would work with him.

Because of that, Evelyn's longtime dream of flying would come true!

Chapter 8

Boarding House Days

The Sharps' home in Ord was a two-story boarding house and café. The family lived in the back rooms downstairs.

They rented out the rest of the bedrooms to other people for a week, a month, or longer. The family had run boarding houses like that in other towns where they lived. Such rooming houses were very common in the early 1900s.

High-Flying Boarder

Starting around 1933 or 1934, a man named Jack Jefford rented a room in the Sharps' house. He usually stayed there two or three times a week.

Jefford and his brother had a flight school

business. Jack kept three small airplanes at Ord's airfield. His brother kept other planes several miles away at the Broken Bow airfield.

Jack Jefford was an excellent pilot and flight instructor. He gave flying lessons in Ord, Broken Bow, and other towns in Central Nebraska.

However, few people had any money in the mid-1930s. So he had only a few students who could afford to pay for lessons.

Jefford often ate at the Sharps' café. He was popular there. Sometimes he entertained people with his flying adventures. Evelyn loved to listen to his stories while she helped cook and clean.

At those times, Evelyn probably remembered her own childhood dream of wanting to "drive" an airplane. She also knew her family did not have money for flying lessons, especially for her, a girl only fourteen- or fifteen-years-old!

A Dream Come True

Then one day, probably in late 1934 or early 1935, Evelyn overheard her father and Jefford talking. The pilot owed money on his planes. He also owed money for his room and board, and he could not pay his bills.

But Jefford had an idea! He knew that Evelyn loved airplanes. So he told John Sharp that he would teach Evelyn to fly—for free—if the Sharps would let him pay his board bill that way—and if Evelyn wanted to learn to fly.

Of course, she did! Evelyn had overheard the men talking. She could not stop herself from saying, "I sure would like to!"

Then she held her breath. What would her father say?

She knew her family needed the board money to pay their own bills. They could not afford to make such a deal. How could she even dream of such a thing?

But Evelyn did SO want to fly in an airplane! More than that, Jack Jefford was not just offering to take her for a plane ride. He was willing to TEACH her—a teenage girl—to fly a plane!

Flying had always been her dream.

To her amazement and joy, Evelyn heard her father agree to Jack Jefford's offer!

Evelyn was so excited that she did not know what to do! She was going to learn to fly an airplane! She could not believe her luck! Her dream was coming true!

At that moment, Evelyn probably had no idea that flying would lead her on to so many other dreams and other goals.

Chapter 9

A Natural-Born Pilot

How anxious Evelyn must have been, waiting for her flying lessons to begin—and wondering if they ever would!

Then, on February 4, 1935, Jefford began to teach her to fly. She was only 15.

Jefford started Evelyn flying in his little two-passenger plane called a **Flyabout**.

Evelyn kept a scrapbook and a journal on tablet paper of her flying adventures. She was also required to keep an official pilot's **logbook** of her flights and training.

Sometimes she flew in the little Flyabout. Sometimes she flew in Jefford's **Curtiss Robin** plane. Still other times, she flew in his five-person plane called a **Stinson-Detroiter.**

When she flew that bigger plane, her father sometimes rode along. When other students took lessons in the bigger plane, Evelyn often rode along, too, to learn things with them.

Evelyn always had a dog when she lived in Ord. At least one of those dogs, Scottie, often flew with her.

Evelyn wearing **jodhpurs** pants (such as those often worn by pilots, horse riders, and military people of the times) holding one of her dogs, possibly her flying pal Scottie (Mary Farmer Palmer Collection, Courtesy Palmer Family)

Fly Right

Evelyn loved flying, and Jack Jefford was a great flight instructor. But he could not always be there to teach her. At times, he needed to take jobs flying in other parts of the country. Then he could not come back for several months.

Sometimes Evelyn had to take lessons from other instructors in Grand Island, Lincoln, or other places while Jack was gone.

Her flight instructors taught her how to land in all kinds of situations. She was an excellent student. She always did her best and tried to learn everything she could about flying.

Jefford and others called her a "natural pilot." Even though flying came naturally to her, she still worked hard to do it right every time.

She just loved flying. She could never get enough of it.

Chapter 10

Running Out of Planes

Jack Jefford was still teaching Evelyn to fly. Then he lost one of his planes in a fire. Before long, he took a job at the airport in Hastings and moved his remaining planes away from Ord.

Around that same time, Evelyn heard that another plane she had been using had been destroyed in a crash. She had no instructor and no planes left to fly. She was grounded.

Evelyn was disappointed. Still, she refused to give up her dream. She kept looking for ways to fly again, but she was not finding anything to help her.

She would have to wait her turn to fly in other

planes. Even that would not slow her down. She stayed busy teaching swimming and working. She seemed to be happy doing those other things, but she really wanted to fly!

The people of Ord were very proud of Evelyn. They were proud of what she was trying to do with her life.

The *Ord Quiz* newspaper ran many stories about her. The paper called her a "natural born pilot." That was nice, but she was still a pilot without a plane.

Solo in a "Flying Bathtub"

Then, on March 4, 1936, Jack Jefford came back to town with another plane. He took Evelyn flying in it. It was a stubby, yellow **Aeronca C-3**. They called it "the Flying Bathtub" or "The Jeep."

Evelyn and Jefford made several takeoffs and landings in the Jeep. Then Jefford made her stop the plane on the runway. He got out and told her to take the plane back up in the air by herself. He felt she was ready to **solo** or fly the plane alone!

Evelyn Sharp solos at age 16 in 1936 (left to right: her instructor Jack Jefford, her classmate LaVern Duemey, Evelyn's dog Contact—or possibly Scottie—and Evelyn, standing in front of Jefford's plane, probably the Aeronca C-3 (Photo Courtesy of Diane Ruth Armour Bartels)

In her journal, Evelyn wrote about her solo flight. She said, "I'll never forget the moment I took off. What a thrill."

She flew around the field several times. Then she made what she called "a perfect, three-point landing" on the plane's three balloon tires.

At that point, she had a total of 13 hours of flying time. She would earn many more hours over the next few years, but it would not be easy.

Joining the Club

Soon after Evelyn's solo, Jefford leased land closer to town. He wanted to use that land as an airfield for more planes.

He also started an **aviation** club or flying club. Members included Evelyn, her father, and fifteen other pilots from Ord and nearby towns.

Evelyn was the youngest member. She may even have been the youngest pilot to solo in those days.

Setting New Goals

Soon Evelyn set new goals for herself. Her first goal was to get her "Amateur License" so she could fly longer flights alone.

It did not take her long to get that license. Then she began to work on her next goal. She wanted to get her private pilot's license.

Evelyn was also very busy in school, playing sports, working for her parents, and doing things for her community at that same time. Still, she always had time for anything to do with airplanes.

In 1936, a Flying Circus air show came to town. Other pilots flew in and added to the excitement. Jack Jefford even did some fancy flying for the crowd.

Evelyn may have dreamed of doing the same thing, but she was not yet ready.

Choosing a Career in Flying

In November of that year, the Ord schools helped Evelyn reach one of her flying goals.

During American Education Week, teachers encouraged their senior students to choose a career. Then the students spent a day with a **mentor**, or a person who could help teach them that job.

Evelyn chose the business of aviation. She spent her time with Jack Jefford. That day, the two of them flew to Grand Island. There, Evelyn passed a test and came home with her private pilot's license.

With that license, she could fly any single-engine airplane. She could also take non-paying passengers flying with her.

Her mother became her first passenger. Her father and her dog became her next passengers. Over the years that followed, Evelyn flew a lot, and she often took her dog with her.

She had also set a new goal for herself. She wanted to become the youngest transport (or **commercial**) pilot in the United States. That means she wanted to make flying her business.

For that, she needed to have 200 flying hours total. Then she would have to pass a very difficult test. That would take a great deal of work and preparation.

Chapter 11

The Business of Flying

Flying was more than just Evelyn's dream. She wanted it to be her business. That meant she needed to join the right clubs and groups, too.

She was already a member of the Ord Aviation Club. Soon she joined the Ord Business and Professional Women's Club, as well.

Then, in January 1937, she received an invitation to join the Nebraska **chapter** of a new flying group. That national group was called the **Ninety-Nines** or the **99s**.

Amelia Earhart (pronounced air-heart) was a famous woman pilot from Kansas. She had helped start that national club by inviting all licensed women pilots in the United States to join the club. Ninety-nine women pilots agreed to join, so the club was called the Ninety-Nines.

Earhart was also that national club's first president. She called her 99s an organization of women pilots who wanted "to fly for the fun of it."

(On July 2, 1937, Amelia Earhart, her **navigator** Fred Noonan, and her plane disappeared while on an around-the-world flight. They were never found. Even today, people wonder what happened to them.)

In January 1937, icy blizzard-like weather kept Evelyn from flying to that first Omaha meeting of the Nebraska chapter of the Ninety-Nines. Instead, she and her father drove to Omaha with a local trucker.

Her father went along to make sure that Evelyn was joining a good group. She was. The women there were very serious about flying, too.

At the meeting, Evelyn found herself in very good company. At that time, just 444 licensed women pilots lived in the United States. Only eight of them lived in Nebraska! Evelyn was the youngest Nebraska member.

How exciting it must have been to be with the women pilots of her state. And how wonderful it must have been to be in a group of the most famous women pilots in the country!

High school photo of Evelyn Sharp (Mary Farmer Palmer Collection, Courtesy Palmer Family)

No Wings to Fly

When Evelyn graduated from high school four months later, she was only 17-years-old. By then, she had sixty-two flying hours. She looked forward to adding many more.

Then once again, she found herself with no plane to fly. Another student pilot had crashed the "flying bathtub." Evelyn must have wondered if she would ever fly again.

Finally, in June 1937, Jefford flew back to Ord for a few days. Evelyn flew his new plane, a **Taylor Cub**, a time or two. Sadly, that added only a few more hours to her total.

It looked as if her goal of getting her transport license might not be reachable. Then help came her way.

Let's Make a Deal

John Sharp had done everything he could to try to help his daughter reach her goals. According to some friends of his, he even tried to buy a small plane for her. But he could not afford the payments.

He did not know what to do, so he asked some of the people in Ord for help. Glen Auble's name came up in those talks. Dr. Auble was a businessman, like Evelyn's dad.

Dr. Auble made and sold eyeglasses. In a small town like Ord, he had to do other things, too. He and his brother Jay also sold jewelry and musical instruments in their store.

Dr. Auble loved history, and he loved the town of Ord. He thought very highly of Evelyn who was a good friend of his daughters. Naturally, he wanted to help her and her family.

John Sharp showed Dr. Auble the airplane he wanted to buy for Evelyn. In a report written sometime later, Dr. Auble said that the plane was in such terrible shape that he "was afraid to risk Evelyn's life flying it." He told John Sharp to give up that plane.

Auble said he would help find a new plane for Evelyn. He even said he would ask the people of

Ord to help him make the down payment for her.

Dr. Auble believed Evelyn had the drive to be a history maker. He knew she always set high goals for herself—but realistic goals. They were goals she could reach, with a little help.

The people of Ord could help her make her dreams come true, and she could make the townspeople proud. Everyone would win in such a deal.

Making the Deal

Dr. Auble talked to the business people in Ord. Money was not easy to get, but they agreed to help. They pooled their money together to make a down payment on a brand new plane for her. Dr. Auble paid much of the down payment money himself.

That plane would not be a free gift. There would be conditions to the deal: Evelyn would have to make payments on the plane.

To earn money, she would make personal appearances and do other jobs. She would also give sky rides to earn more flying hours and to promote herself and the town of Ord.

Evelyn agreed to the deal. She said she would pay the town back for the plane and for believing in her.

Teenager Evelyn Sharp would soon have her very own brand new plane! She would work very hard to try to make the payments and to keep her plane, but it would not be easy.

Chapter 12

Hometown Girl and "The Ord"

On August 17, 1937, Jack Jefford called Evelyn and her father. He told them to be ready to fly to Omaha with him the following day.

They were going to go get her new plane—the one the business people of Ord were helping her buy.

That plane was a brand new silver-colored two-person Taylor Cub. Evelyn would call her new plane "The Ord."

She was so excited! There were only seven women in Nebraska at that time who owned and piloted their own airplanes. At seventeen, Evelyn would be one of them, and the youngest!

The next day, Evelyn, her dad, and Jefford flew his plane to Omaha. They went to check out Evelyn's new plane. Then Evelyn and her father climbed into the Taylor Cub and flew west, toward home.

Evelyn's father was pleased with her skills. He saw that she handled the plane very well in the wind. He felt the Taylor Cub was in good hands. He knew his daughter had a real future as a pilot.

Then, about halfway home, the weather turned bad.

The little airplane had no radio. It had no instruments to help the pilot fly in bad weather or at night. Even if it had, Evelyn's license would not allow her to fly in such conditions. She knew she had to land soon.

Stormy Night at a Cemetery

Very soon, twisting winds and bad storms forced Evelyn to land her new plane in farm fields—twice.

The second time she landed, she put her plane

down in a field not far from the town of Aurora—
and just across the road from a country cemetery.

Father and daughter spent a very restless night
in the tiny plane. They had no way to get to a
phone to let people know where they were. And it
was getting dark.

John Sharp tried to sleep in the tiny cramped
plane. But Evelyn was so excited! She just wanted
to talk all night about her new plane.

The storm did not help. Thunder crashed and
lightning flashed. It lit up and shadowed the
tombstones in a spooky way.

When the wind calmed and the rain stopped,
mosquitoes swarmed the plane. Then the storm
raged again.

The young pilot and her father were very tired
and very glad when morning came. It finally
brought clear skies, a good takeoff, and a safe
landing at home.

"The Ord"

Back home, Evelyn had the name "The Ord"

painted on the side of her new plane. That name honored her hometown and the people who had helped her buy her first plane.

The people of Ord loved to see the name of their town on the side of Evelyn's plane. They loved to watch her fly that airplane over the hills.

The people of Ord loved to see Evelyn Sharp, their hometown girl, fly her plane "The Ord" over the hills. (Photo Courtesy of Irene Auble Abernethy)

Giving Sky Rides

Right away, Evelyn started promoting her plane and earning more flight hours. In those days, she often circled the farmyards and landed in the valleys out in the country. There she picked up anyone who wanted to go for a sky ride. Many people looked forward to riding with her and her dog.

Emanuel "Gabe" Lukesh was Evelyn's age. He lived with his family on a farm five miles southwest of Ord. Gabe and his younger brother Richard or "Butch" were musicians. They played trumpets for their father Joe Lukesh and his very popular **polka** band.

Whenever Gabe saw Evelyn flying the hills, he ran out past the hill behind his parents' house. There he watched and waved at her.

If she landed, he climbed into the plane and went for a sky ride with her. Gabe loved to fly with his friend Evelyn—and her dog—over the sandhills. So did many people of the area.

It was good for Evelyn, too. Each flight added flying hours, passenger numbers, and takeoffs and landings to her logbook, as she worked on her goals.

She only had a private pilot's license so she could not yet charge people money for sky rides.

She would need to get a transport license for that.

With her own plane, Evelyn quickly added more flying hours and 80 more passengers to her totals. She often took her dog Scottie with her. They became famous.

Evelyn and one of her dogs, probably her famous flying companion Scottie (Photo Courtesy of Irene Auble Abernethy)

Chapter 13

Grand Celebrations, Big Problems

The news about the girl pilot from Ord—and her dog—spread across Nebraska and into nearby states. Many people wanted to see Evelyn fly.

On September 15, 1937, she became the first pilot to land at the brand new $400,000 Arrasmith Air Field at Grand Island, Nebraska.

Flying visits to other towns followed. With each visit, she passed out tickets, postcards, and ribbons. Those gave her name and said she was "America's Youngest Licensed Pilot." They also featured pictures of her, "The Ord" plane, and her flying dog Scottie.

More Instruction and Visits

All those flying visits and hours in the air helped make Evelyn famous and added to her totals. Before long, she had the 200 hours she needed to take the test for her transport license.

Unfortunately, she did not have the instructor she needed to prepare her for the test. Jack Jefford had taken another job, as a pilot in Alaska. So Evelyn looked for another teacher to help her reach her goal.

In the meantime, she went back to Grand Island for the opening of Arrasmith Air Field. There the celebration started with a very special **telegraph** message. That **telegram** came from Orville Wright—one of the Wright Brothers who had been the first pilots to fly in America.

The celebration then spread downtown. There Evelyn signed ribbons and postcards at the Wolbach Store at 3rd and Pine Streets. (Some of those items were kept on display there in a glass case for thirty years or more.)

That evening, more than 2,300 people paid $1.50 each to dance in an airplane **hangar** at the Air Field in honor of Evelyn. About 700 of them could not even get into the crowded building, so they danced outside instead. Indoors or out, everyone seemed to have a grand time.

Testing—Out!

A few days later, Evelyn began working with another instructor to get ready to take her transport (now called a commercial) pilot test. If she passed that test and got her transport license, she could charge money for sky rides. That would help her pay off her plane.

She really wanted that license, but it was a very hard one to get. Test subjects included questions about weather, **navigation**, weight and balance, airplane engine work, and airplane construction.

Evelyn passed parts of the exam, but she did not pass it all. In the end, she failed the transport test!

In big black letters, newspapers reported she had "flunked" the test. However, those papers also said the transport exam was extremely tough. Many men had failed it the first time they took it.

Still, Evelyn was very ashamed of her failure. She felt she had let down the people of Ord and all her other fans.

She promised to take more training. She said she would try to retake the test in three months. She promised to do her best to pass next time.

She really wanted to pass that transport test. She needed to pass it, so she could get that license and charge people for sky rides. She knew that was the best way—and maybe the only way—she could make enough money to keep flying.

Chapter 14

Resetting Goals

After failing the transport test, Evelyn could not make the payments on her brand new Taylor Cub. She was in danger of losing her new plane.

She had no way to pay her bills or to pay another instructor to teach her what she needed to know for that exam. And she could not retake the test for three months. That was too long.

She was caught in a no-win situation. She did not know what to do, and her family could not help her.

That January of 1938 was a very sad time for her. Unable to make her payments, she had to give up her brand new airplane. There was nothing she could do about it.

After losing her plane, she still kept busy looking for other ways to fly and to pass the transport test. She still wanted to go on with the business of flying.

Finally, she found what she was looking for—a flying school in Lincoln. There she could take classes and keep working to pass the test. She could also meet other goals.

There was still one big problem, though. She did not have the money she needed to take the classes at the flying school.

Another Dance, To Fly

Evelyn told the people of Ord about her problems, her dreams, and her goals.

Again Dr. Glen Auble and the town of Ord came to her rescue. They held a benefit dance to raise money for her schooling.

People came to the dance to help her, a girl who dreamed of flying and who set goals to get where she wanted to be.

Evelyn (second from left), Dr. Glen Auble (just to the right of Evelyn's dog), and four other Auble family members (Photo Courtesy of Irene Auble Abernethy)

The dance raised enough money for Evelyn to go to the Lincoln Airplane and Flying School in January of 1938. She then moved there and stayed with a family who had relatives in Ord.

She loved the hands-on courses offered at the flight school. She practiced flying, studied airplanes, and took apart and put back together the inner workings of planes and engines.

The Pride of Airplane School

Evelyn was the only girl among 75 boys at the Lincoln aviation school. Other girls had started classes there, but they had quit along the way. But Evelyn was no quitter.

James Misko was vice-president of the First National Bank in Ord at that time. One day he visited the Lincoln Airplane and Flying School. He asked the man in charge there about Evelyn.

The superintendent told Misko the following: "Miss Sharp is a different type of girl. She entered the school with the expectation of making good. She is a brilliant student, hard work[ing], attends strictly to business [and] command[s] respect of everyone. She is the pride of the school."

Evelyn really liked the school, too. She wrote and told a friend what she was learning in class and about her new friends in Lincoln. She also talked about her hopes, dreams, and goals.

Evelyn enjoyed life. She wanted a future, with a husband and a family of her own. Even more, she wanted a future flying airplanes. She would continue to work hard and stay on that course to make her dreams come true.

Chapter 15

On Stage, On Screen, and In the Air

April and May of 1938 were very busy months for Evelyn.

In April she returned to Grand Island. There she was a special guest at the Capitol Theater for a movie called *Test Pilot*. It featured some of the most famous movie stars in Hollywood—Clark Gable, Myrna Loy, and Spencer Tracy.

Huge crowds showed up to see both the movie and the girl pilot from Ord. Later she received a telegram and a letter from those stars. They thanked her for helping to make their movie a success! She made visits to other theaters to promote their airplane movies as well.

A two-part ad for Evelyn's visit to an area town and for a theater showing an airplane movie of the time (Mary Farmer Palmer Collection, Courtesy Palmer Family)

A few weeks later, on a very lucky Friday the 13th of May in 1938, Evelyn retook the transport test and received her license. That made her the only licensed female commercial pilot in the state of Nebraska. She could then charge money to take passengers flying—but she had no plane!

A week later, on May 19, she landed in Grand Island for another big event. It celebrated the 20th Anniversary of Air Mail in America. She had to borrow a plane from a friend to make that flight.

Crowds cheered as she took off from the

Grand Island airfield. In her borrowed plane, she carried a big bag of special mail for Ord and other towns—more than 2,500 pieces of mail.

She made many stops and speeches in central Nebraska, as the only female airmail pilot to fly in the state during that event.

Fan Mail

Evelyn sent and received her own share of fan mail in the days that followed. She even received a very special letter from Eleanor Roosevelt, the wife of President Franklin Roosevelt.

Mrs. Roosevelt had been a good friend of one of Evelyn's heroes—the Kansas pilot, Amelia Earhart—and had even flown with her. Evelyn was proud and happy to receive that airmail letter.

For the rest of her life, Evelyn wrote and sent many letters. She stayed in touch with family, friends, and her ever-growing list of fans across the country and beyond.

Chapter 16

Return to Sky Riding

With her new transport license, Evelyn was able to start charging people for sky rides. She borrowed another airplane and began earning money for a new plane.

Stover Deats from the Grand Island airfield had been one of her flight instructors. In August, he sold the Sharp family an old Curtiss Robin airplane. Once again, Evelyn had her own wings.

According to her logbook, she took thousands of people for sky rides across Nebraska during the next two years. By October 1939, her record book would list more than 5,000 names.

Evelyn charged 75¢ or $1.00 for each ride,

depending upon the rider's age. That was a lot of money in those days.

Some of the things Evelyn and John Sharp gave out during sky rides and visits: Evelyn Sharp tags and sky ride tickets. (Photos from the Irene Auble Abernethy, Diane Ruth Armour Bartels, and Mary Farmer Palmer Collections)

It took lots of money to fly and maintain a plane—money for bank payments, fuel, storage, and more. That old Curtiss Robin plane often needed repair or replacement parts, too.

There were other costs, as well. Often her dad followed her flights across the state in his truck. He watched over her, helped her with repairs, put ads in the newspapers, sold tickets, and printed and passed out cards, tags, and other information about her. All that took money, too.

To Pay the Bills

Evelyn and her father were still on the road or in the air giving sky rides through 1939. Evelyn's mother Mary stayed in Ord. She tried to run the family's many businesses.

Mary tried hard, but she had too much to do. She could not handle everything. Soon the family could not make their payments. They lost their café. Mary had to go to work for someone else.

Evelyn's sky riding money had to make the payments on the plane. It also had to help support her family and pay even more of the family's bills.

Evelyn wanted to do more with her flying, but she did not know what more she could do. She needed to talk to other women pilots to find out what they were doing.

Chapter 17

"Baby Flier"

On March 1, 1939, Evelyn and her mom drove to Fort Worth, Texas, in very bad weather. They went to the national aviation meeting of the Ninety-Nines (99s), or women pilots.

At the meeting, Evelyn met many famous pilots, including Jacqueline Cochran. The people there knew Cochran as a female test pilot who often set air speed records.

In just a few years, Cochran would become president of the Ninety-Nines. She would also become a very important person in Evelyn's life.

Several other Ninety-Nine members attended the 1939 conference, too. A newspaper reporter took a picture of Evelyn there. He called her the "baby flier" among the older women pilots. She was the youngest of the 34 women in America who could then charge passengers to fly in their planes.

Evelyn came home all excited. She knew she wanted to do a lot more with her flying skills than just take people for sky rides.

She wondered what else a teenage pilot could do. Could she teach other people how to fly? She wanted to find out.

Something Old, Something New

A few months before, Evelyn had called the Lincoln aviation school. She had asked them what she needed to do to become an instructor.

She did not find out what she wanted to know, at that time, but she did hear two amazing things. First, she heard that the school had bought "The Ord." That was the plane she had once owned.

That plane was very special to her. She felt she had to go see it again. She went to the school and flew her old plane one last time.

Then she heard the second amazing thing. The owner of the Lincoln flying school was then in Washington, D.C. He had gone there to talk with the government about starting a new kind of air school to teach more men and women to fly.

That new kind of schooling would be called the **Civilian Pilot Training Program** or **CPTP**.

The man from the Lincoln flying school had many reasons for wanting to start that new flight school: Aviation was a growing business. Many people wanted to learn to fly, but few people had the money for schooling. Also there were very few good flight instructors available.

At that time, there was a war going on in Europe, too. The government feared the U.S. would soon have to join that war. If that happened, the military would need more American men to pilot warplanes. The CPTP could teach lots more men to fly, to get ready for war.

Evelyn waited to see what would happen with

the new CPTP flying schools. While she waited, she kept working to support herself, her plane, and her family.

She had no choice. She had to keep making barnstorming tours across Nebraska. She had to give sky rides to anyone who could pay for them.

Meeting Aunt Elsie

In late July of 1939, while she was giving sky rides at North Platte, Evelyn met a family friend named Elsie Rick. John Sharp said to call the lady "Aunt Elsie." Mary Sharp, Evelyn's mom, even drove in from Ord for that family get-together.

Evelyn and Aunt Elsie looked a lot alike. Even so, Evelyn did not know if they were really related or if the woman was just a family friend.

Evelyn took Elsie for sky rides. They had a great time together and became very good friends.

All too soon, Aunt Elsie had to go home to New York. She invited Evelyn to visit her there. They wrote and visited each other whenever they could over the years that followed.

Chapter 18

Damages and Repairs

One day while Evelyn was taking off on another sky ride, her plane was damaged by tall grass on an uneven field. The expensive repairs took a long time.

Once again she was left with no plane, just when she needed it most. So in September 1939, she bought a newer Curtiss Robin plane.

She used the new one while the old one was in for repairs. But soon she realized she could not make the payments on that new plane and had to give it up.

Around that time, things went from bad to even worse. Mary Sharp was making very little money in Ord. Evelyn and her father were working part-time at the Grand Island airfield.

Evelyn worried about her family and about what to do with her own life. All that worry probably led to the serious asthma attack she had in January 1940.

She had to stay flat on her back in bed for many days. It took time to regain her strength. She felt her dreams were going nowhere.

The Winds of Change

Then, one very windy March day, Evelyn looked out her window near the Grand Island airfield and saw something very strange.

She saw a tiny yellow plane with its nose to the ground and its tail in the air. A man was trying to hold down his plane and keep the wind from destroying it.

Without thinking, Evelyn tore out of the building. She ran across the fields, climbed a tall fence, jumped a ditch, and ran to help the man.

Together she and the pilot held down the

plane until more people came to help them. They kept the wind from tearing the little plane apart. Even so, the plane was damaged. Both wing tips were bent. The propeller also needed to be replaced.

The pilot ordered a new propeller. Then he took a bus home to Iowa, leaving the plane at the airfield. He told Evelyn that she could fly the plane for a month if she would have it fixed first. He also wanted her to fly it to Lincoln for him later.

Evelyn and a friend fixed and replaced the damaged parts. Then she took it for a spin. The little plane was not very powerful, but at least, she had something to fly for a while.

Back on Course

In mid-April, Evelyn took her dog Scottie and flew the little plane to Lincoln. She stayed over and spent two days practicing flying there at Lindbergh and Arrow Airfields. (Lindbergh Airfield was named for Charles Lindbergh, a world-famous pilot who learned to fly in Lincoln.)

Evelyn decided to stay in Lincoln a while longer. She wanted to do more flying and wanted to renew her transport license. While there, she also worked, studied, gave interviews, and helped start a new flying club.

In June of 1940, she passed the test to become a flight instructor. She was 20 years old. By then, she had been flying for five years. She had more than 800 flight hours and had taken more than 5,000 passengers on sky rides.

She felt she was ready to become a flight instructor. She looked for more information about the new Civilian Pilot Training Program (or CPTP). At the same time, her father also sent out letters to help her get a flying job.

Soon Evelyn had a new career teaching flying.

Chapter 19

Flying for the CPTP

Evelyn heard about an opening at a Civilian Pilot Training Program school in Mitchell, South Dakota. She flew there and applied for the position. The very next day she had the job as a temporary teacher.

At that time, she became the youngest flight instructor in the country. After that, she took a job as a CPTP flight instructor at Spearfish, South Dakota.

Her parents and her dog Scottie moved there to be closer to her. They all lived together in a trailer near the airfield.

Evelyn taught flying at Spearfish for the rest

of 1940. Most of her students were men, but each CPTP class was supposed to have at least one female student, too.

Many of her male students went on to fly for the military. She even met some of them again a few years later during the war.

Evelyn with a Douglas B-18 (bomber) crew, at Spearfish (South Dakota) in 1940, while she was teaching many men and a few women to fly for the CPTP or Civilian Pilot Training Program (Photo Courtesy of Diane Ruth Armour Bartels)

More Goals

In January 1941, Evelyn and her family moved to Bakersfield, California. There she taught CPTP flying classes and set more goals.

Mary and John Sharp, Evelyn's adopted parents, 1941, in Bakersfield, California (Mary Farmer Palmer Collection, Courtesy Palmer Family)

Evelyn also took more classes herself. She worked to get two more licenses. One of those was to teach **aerobatic**s. That was a special and very skillful kind of flying. With that license, she could also teach advanced aviation classes.

The other license she earned was an **instrument rating**. That meant she could fly using the flight instruments in her plane, even if she could not see out because of heavy clouds or bad weather.

A magazine of that time then carried a story about her. It said she was the youngest of the ten licensed women flight instructors in the United States. (By the time she quit teaching for the CPTP in late 1942, she had taught more than 350 students to fly. Most of those students were men.)

Soon she had a total of 2,000 flight hours of her own. Her new boss had nothing but good things to say about his new instructor.

Everybody seemed to like Evelyn. She had brown eyes and brown hair and was pretty and popular. She had lots of friends but did not smoke, drink, or date her students.

Evelyn was very athletic and energetic. So happy and excited about life and flying was she, that she sometimes walked upside down on her hands or turned cartwheels to burn up energy.

She loved her job, but when she was flying,

she was all business and was very serious. Everyone knew she had real barnstorming skills, but she was never foolish or careless.

She was always prepared for any emergency, whether she was flying alone or with a student. She would NEED to be prepared. War was coming.

This Means WAR!

On December 7, 1941, Evelyn was in the air over California with a student pilot. On that day, Japan (a country in Asia) bombed the United States Navy base at Pearl Harbor, Hawaii.

Hawaii was not yet a U.S. state. It was then a group of islands protected by the United States of America. (Hawaii is in the Pacific Ocean, thousands of miles away from either Japan or California.)

At the time of the Pearl Harbor attack, another flight instructor named Cornelia Fort was in the air OVER Pearl Harbor. (She would later become a good friend of Evelyn's.)

Seeing the attack coming, Cornelia grabbed her plane's controls out of her student's hands. Quickly she flew the plane away from the Japanese warplanes and the harbor.

The attack on Pearl Harbor caused the United States to go to war against Japan. Within days, Germany, a country in Europe, also declared war on the U.S.

Soon many countries all over the world took sides in that new war called World War II or the Second World War.

Moving Planes Inland

After the attack on Pearl Harbor, the airfield at Bakersfield became very busy. Thousands of American soldiers and military planes took over the area.

The U.S. government told civilian pilots they had to stay inland, at least 150 miles away from the Pacific Ocean. All civilian planes and airfields had to be moved away from the coast.

Evelyn's boss moved his planes inland to the

high desert. He re-opened his flight school at a place called Lone Pine, California. Evelyn and her dog Scottie moved to Lone Pine, but her parents stayed in Bakersfield.

Evelyn was beginning a new chapter in her adult life. Before long, she would be moving planes for the military. The military needed many planes to fight in such a huge world war.

Chapter 20

Top Secret Pilot Projects

After moving to Lone Pine, Evelyn received a telegram from Jacqueline Cochran. They knew each other from the women pilots' group, the Ninety-Nines.

That telegram invited Evelyn to become part of a special pilot program. Cochran wanted to gather the most experienced women pilots to help America win the war. She wanted Evelyn in that group.

Cochran did not want American women to fly in combat. She wanted those pilots to deliver warplanes from factories where they were made to U.S. air bases and sometimes to fly them across the Pacific and Atlantic oceans.

That moving of planes from one place (or from one base) to another was called ferrying planes or transporting them. New planes had to be moved to make them ready and available for war.

If women pilots transported those planes, then that would free up more men pilots to fly the planes into combat. Cochran and other women pilots were already transporting some planes to or around England. Cochran wanted women pilots to be able to do that in the United States, as well.

Other people had similar ideas and plans. Even Eleanor Roosevelt, the President's wife, saw the value of women pilots.

Newspapers quoted her as saying, "This is not a time when women should be patient. We are in a war, and we need to fight it with every weapon possible. WOMEN PILOTS are a weapon waiting to be used."

The Meeting

To get her own pilot project going, Cochran

met privately with President Franklin Roosevelt, his wife Eleanor, and General Henry Arnold.

General Henry "Hap" Arnold was in charge of the Army Air Forces. (Not long after World War II ended, the Army Air Forces became the U.S. Air Force, a separate branch of the military.)

First Lady Eleanor Roosevelt often sat in on meetings with, or for, her husband. She met with important people, visited hard-to-get-to places, and did lots of busy work for him, because he was crippled with a disease called **polio**.

During her meeting with the Roosevelts and General Arnold, Cochran explained her idea of how American women pilots could transport warplanes to where they were needed. The group listened but did not come to an agreement. Many things needed to be decided first.

At that time, General Arnold was not sure if he even wanted American women flying for the Army Air Forces. The government was not ready to commit to Cochran's idea.

Jacqueline Cochran decided to send telegrams anyway. In those telegrams, she invited the most experienced American women pilots to fly with her to help their country. Then Cochran returned to England to see what she could do there.

Not the Right Time

Although proud and excited to receive an invitation, Evelyn decided not to join Cochran's program. She still had a contract to teach pilots how to fly. She decided to keep teaching and to wait and see what would happen.

In between classes, she exercised and played sports to stay healthy. But she was also sad and lonely. Her parents had moved away to Nevada. And Scottie, her favorite dog, had been run over by a car and killed.

Before long, Evelyn found another puppy. She named him Shanty McTavish. She took him flying with her. He also went with her on her next career move. That move came very soon.

Chapter 21

"The Originals"

Before long, Evelyn heard from another woman pilot and some other generals. They wanted to use American women pilots to help in the war by moving warplanes, too.

They sent a telegram to Evelyn and to at least 83 other women pilots. Each of those women had 500 or more flying hours.

Those telegrams invited the best women pilots to apply to be part of an Army-related group that would fly new planes from U.S. airplane factories to bases in the U.S. and Canada.

That was not Jackie Cochran's program, but it was similar to hers. This one belonged to another female pilot, Nancy Harkness Love. Love called her program the Women's Auxiliary Ferrying Squadron, or the WAFS.

By that time, Evelyn was at a point where she could end her CPTP teaching contract. She did that and became one of the first women to join the original WAFS program.

She would also be one of the youngest and most experienced of its pilots. But first, she had to be accepted into the program.

Meeting the Requirements

To be accepted into the WAFS program, Evelyn and those other women pilots had to have the following **qualifications** and more:

- Be an American citizen, 21 to 35 years old.
- Pass an Army medical exam.
- Have graduated from high school.
- Have a total of 500 or more flying hours.
- Have flown airplanes with high-powered engines.

Few women pilots met all those qualifications.

Evelyn did. She was a high school graduate and not quite 22 years of age, so she was one of the youngest pilots to apply.

She was small, only 5'4" tall, and weighed about 115 pounds, but that was within the size limits. Full of energy and very athletic, she easily passed the Army medical exam.

She also had almost 3,000 flying hours—well over the required 500 hours—and some of those were in higher-powered planes!

After passing all the tests, she became the 17th woman pilot accepted into the WAFS program. That happened on October 20, 1942, her real birthday (though she did not know it then).

At first, there were 28 women pilots accepted into that first group, but three of them were soon cut from the program. The remaining 25 came to be called "The **Originals**."

They were then sent to Newcastle Army Air Base at Wilmington, Delaware. There they learned do things "the Army Way."

One of "The Originals" or Evelyn Sharp in her WAFS **uniform** (Women's Auxiliary Ferrying Squadron), 1941, Newcastle Army Air Base, Delaware - The pen writing across her shoulder says, "Your loving granddaughter, As always, Evelyn."

Over the years, Evelyn's family combined their photos. Then two or three copies of this "favorite" picture ended up in a suitcase full of Evelyn's personal and family photos, letters, and more. That suitcase was later handed down to Evelyn's cousin Mary Farmer Palmer.

All her life, Mary Farmer Palmer idolized her (adopted) first cousin Evelyn, who had been seven years older. Mary treasured the suitcase collection. She and her two sons were kind enough to share its contents with others, including this author, who also admired Evelyn. (Mary Farmer Palmer Collection, Courtesy Palmer Family)

Chapter 22

"The Army Way"

Nancy Love's women pilots were not really in the military. They could not get military benefits. Even so, they still had to learn to do everything the Army way.

First, they had to train as if they were soldiers. They had to know and follow military rules. They had to know how to use and handle weapons, stand guard, march, and much more.

Then they needed to learn how to fly several different kinds of military planes. They had to know each kind of plane very well. They also had to learn about new aircraft as they came along.

In those early days of the war, very few

planes had radios or instruments. Pilots really had to know how to read maps, recognize landmarks, understand the weather, and do a lot more.

In Uniform

At first, those women pilots were called **trainees**. When they flew or worked on planes, they wore one-piece military flying suits or jump suits in summer and long-zippered leather pants and jackets in winter.

At times, they also wore goggles, leather helmets, facemasks, lined gloves, and heavy wool-lined boots. That was for the bitter cold of flying in an open **cockpit** airplane. Of course, they also needed a **parachute**, too, in case of an emergency.

On Their Best Behavior

The women pilots often dressed in gear similar to that of the men. Still, they were expected to act like proper ladies at all times. They were not to smoke, drink, do any improper things, or even eat at the same table in the **mess hall** with any men who were not their husbands.

Usually, the only place that men and women pilots could be together was at the officers' club. There they could talk, dance, see movies, play cards, or take part in some other social games.

Evelyn, all dressed up to meet friends at the officers' club (Mary Farmer Palmer Collection, Courtesy Palmer Family)

Even there, the women had to be on their best behavior. If they broke the rules, they could be kicked out of the program. They could even cause the whole program to fail.

Evelyn was pretty and very well liked. She had trained lots of military pilots to fly in the CPTP. She had many good friends among them. She liked to dance and go to the movies with some of those male officers. However, she was not interested in getting married yet. Flying was her life.

WAFS in uniforms (Evelyn is second from the left) (Photo Courtesy, National Museum of the U.S. Air Force)

After passing all their tests, those women trainees were called WAFS. Then they wore a classy new gray-green uniform. The uniform had a jacket, a shirt, a skirt or slacks, a cap, special military patches, and silver-wing pins. They also had warm flight suits.

The Ground Rules

The ferrying pilots had strict flying rules: They could only fly if the ground could be seen very clearly from the air, and they could only fly during the daytime. Those and other rules kept them from flying very much in winter or in rainy or cloudy weather—even if they had an instrument rating, like Evelyn did.

After delivering a plane to a base, the WAFS had to take a public plane, train, or bus back to their home base. They were not allowed to fly in a military plane with men, unless ordered to do so by their commanders.

They did get one special favor though. When flying back to a base, they could "**bump**" or take the seat of anyone on a commercial plane—anyone except the President of the United States or his

cabinet members.

Back Home on Base

Back on the bases, the women lived in Army **barracks**. Barracks are buildings where soldiers sleep, usually in big long rows of beds or cots. Those buildings often had a group shower and bathroom area, with very little privacy.

A housemother watched over the WAFS members in their barracks. Men were not allowed inside the building. Evelyn's new dog Shanty was not even supposed to be there, but no one stopped him.

While in training, the women pilots received $150 a month. Their pay went up to $250 a month after they graduated from training. From that money, they had to pay for their meals, room and board, and uniforms.

They paid 75 cents a day for their rooms.

How strange it must have seemed to Evelyn to be paying her own board bills to fly the military planes. Perhaps that reminded her of when Jack

Jefford could not pay his own board bill—and how Evelyn had been given that golden chance to fly and make her dreams come true.

Everything in her life seemed to come back to flying.

Evelyn in uniform at the WAFS' barracks door (Mary Farmer Palmer Collection, Courtesy Palmer Family)

Chapter 23

Learning the Truth

In November of 1942, Evelyn's "Aunt Elsie" came to the WAFS base to visit her. Elsie and Evelyn looked so much alike that many people called them mother and daughter.

Evelyn corrected those people, but even she was not sure how Aunt Elsie was related to her. Still, there was no doubt Elsie was very proud of her "niece" and of the work she did.

The two of them had a great visit before Evelyn was called away to fly a ferrying mission. Elsie left then, too, to spend Thanksgiving with friends before returning to her home in New York.

Evelyn in her **Air Transport Command** (or **ATC**) jacket and goggles - Nancy Love's WAFS and Jackie Cochran's women pilots were both part of the larger ATC group. (Mary Farmer Palmer Collection, Courtesy Palmer Family)

The Best Job in the World

During the next months, Nancy Love's WAFS delivered many planes across the U.S. and Canada. So did Jackie Cochran's new women ferrying pilots. Her program had finally been accepted, too.

They were two separate ferrying groups, but

they were both a part of the Air Transport Command or ATC. (The government and the military use lots of abbreviations.)

Evelyn and the other WAFS then flew some of the same planes the men did. But the lady fliers could not yet fly the bigger or faster warplanes.

Still, Evelyn loved what she was doing. She thought her new flying job was the most enjoyable one in the world!

The Truth

In late January 1943, Evelyn ferried a plane to Canada. She came back through New York and stopped to see Aunt Elsie. They went out to eat.

Then Elsie finally told Evelyn the truth. Elsie Rick had once been known as Elsie Haeske Crouse. She was really Evelyn's birth mother—not her aunt!

What a surprise that was for Evelyn! How happy she was to find out the truth. She had always wondered why she never looked like her parents—John and Mary Sharp. As a child, she had even secretly wondered if she had been adopted.

Evelyn loved her "Aunt Elsie" very much. She even continued to call her by that name. They were more than family. They would also be good friends for the rest of Evelyn's life.

Evelyn was not angry with any of her parents for keeping the secret from her. She loved them all very much. She also appreciated everything they had done for her all her life.

Evelyn in uniform with "Aunt Elsie" in January 1943 - Aunt Elsie (Haeske Crouse) Rick was Evelyn's birth mother. (Mary Farmer Palmer Collection, Courtesy Palmer Family)

Evelyn later told two of her WAFS roommates about her real mother Elsie. Evelyn was so happy to find out she had two mothers and a father—and that all of them loved her very much.

Evelyn hated to leave her real mother in New York, but she was eager to get back to work flying planes. The new WAFS program was changing, and she needed to know more about those changes.

WAFS at Long Beach, California (Army Air Base) (left to right) Barbara Towne (standing), Cornelia Fort (sitting on wing), Evelyn Sharp, Barbara Erickson, and Bernice Batten (Photo Courtesy, The Woman's Collection, Texas Woman's University, Denton, Texas; also, Courtesy, National Museum of the U.S. Air Force)

Back to Work

About that time, Nancy Love split up her 25 "original" WAFS into smaller groups. Each small group was then sent to a different base in the U.S.

Jacqueline Cochran's women ferry pilots then joined them at those bases.

Evelyn went to the base at Long Beach with four other WAFS: Barbara Erickson, Cornelia Fort, Barbara Towne, and Bernice Batten. (Her new dog Shanty went to live with her parents in Nevada.)

The new jobs at Long Beach kept the fly girls busy. One of the first things they had to learn was how to use the radios that came in the newer planes.

Those two-way radios were not for fun or for listening to music. They were used only for important things, such as contacting air bases, getting weather conditions, or reporting mechanical problems.

Having and knowing how to use a radio in an

airplane could be the key to a pilot's survival.

(Sadly, America's favorite woman pilot, Amelia Earhart, learned that lesson too late when she and her airplane disappeared over the ocean and were never found.)

With the world at war, Evelyn also needed to learn many survival skills. She needed to know how to use a life raft, oxygen masks, parachute, pistols, machine guns, and more. She needed to be prepared for anything.

She also needed to stay fit. That was no problem. She still loved sports and doing lots of athletic things in her free time.

Chapter 24

Women Pilots in the News

The public and the Army all wanted to know more about the women pilots flying for the Army Air Forces. People especially wanted to know how well they could do a man's job.

People also wanted to know who they were. Many of them were young and pretty. Some were single. Some were married. Some were even moms.

Reporters wrote stories and took pictures of the women pilots. As one of the youngest of those pilots, Evelyn had her picture taken often.

Other WAFS showed up regularly in the pictures, too, including Jackie Cochran and Nancy

Love, the leaders of those women pilots. So did Barbara Erickson and Cornelia Fort, two of Evelyn's friends who lived in the same barracks with her.

The Job

Those stories and pictures told about the women pilots and how they transported new planes for the Army Air Forces. The stories said the women pilots even served as test pilots for new planes fresh from the factory and for repaired ones from other places.

If planes were going to have problems, those troubles often showed up in the first few flights, usually during takeoffs and landings.

Some stories told how women fliers towed targets and banners across the sky while men practiced shooting at those targets with machine guns or **artillery** and real **ammunition**.

Other stories noted that the women fliers did other jobs, too. They did demonstrations, taught flying, flew weather planes, flew searchlight missions, and served as pilots for some officers.

A Work Force of Women

Often the news reporters talked about the men going off to war. They also talked about how more and more women were working away from home for the first time in their lives. The women did that to fill the jobs the men had left. Those jobs were important to keep our country running.

Women were even working in the factories to make new planes. More and more of those new planes needed to be made, so more women were hired.

The military also needed more women pilots to transport such aircraft to bases across America or to ports where the planes were sent so they could be shipped or flown overseas to war.

Women from all over the country saw those jobs as an exciting way to help America with the war effort. The women were helping just like the men had been doing. In that way, they could all make a little money and do important work that needed doing—all at the same time.

Before the war ended, more than 25,000 women applied to become transport or ferry pilots. The Army accepted some of those women and sent them for training. Only a few of them would pass and later become WAFS or other ATC pilots.

As those new women pilots were learning their craft and the Army way of doing things, Jacqueline Cochran and Nancy Love's women fliers continued to set the standards for flying excellence.

Chapter 25

"Best of the Best"

Less experienced women pilots could fly the smaller, slower, or older planes. Only the best or most experienced WAFS members could fly the brand new kinds of planes—but first, each of those pilots had to **qualify** (test out) or prove they could handle such aircraft.

The leaders of the women pilots, Nancy Love and Jacqueline Cochran, first tested their skills in the newer, more complicated aircraft.

Those warplanes included some attack planes and **pursuit planes** (sometimes also called fighter or escort planes), as well as some of the big **cargo planes**, and even some of the bombers.

After one or both of those leaders passed the flight tests, then Evelyn, the other WAFS members, and the next group of women pilots took their turns trying to test out in each model.

If they passed, they were qualified to fly that type of plane to bases across the country and to Canada. Each pilot could only transport the kinds of planes that she was qualified to fly.

To Fly the Big Birds

Evelyn flew whatever planes the military told her to fly, to wherever they wanted her to take the aircraft. She loved her job, and she loved to fly any plane—any time.

But she also wanted to fly the newer, faster, more powerful planes just being developed. To do that, she had to study a lot. She had to know all the controls and instruments in each of those planes and what each one did.

She also had to learn everything she could about each plane, and she had to fly as much as possible. So she kept her name on the "ready to fly" list at all times.

She qualified in and flew some of the big, heavy cargo or transport planes that carried men and vehicles. Their model names often started with the letter C, such as the C-47 (also called a DC-3).

She also qualified in and flew some of the bombers. Their model names started with the letter B, such as the B-25 Mitchell bombers.

She even qualified in and flew some of the attack planes. Their names started with the letter A, such as the A-20 Havoc.

Evelyn became one of only three women who were then qualified to fly the A-20, a plane some people called "a mankiller." She also became the first woman to fly that model from coast to coast.

But she loved flying pursuit planes even more. Their names often started with P, such as the P-40 Warhawk and the P-47 Thunderbolt.

In Pursuit of Faster Planes

Those were great planes, but some other pursuit planes—especially the P-51 Mustang and the P-38 Lightning—worked even better for longer missions.

Evelyn could not wait to test out and fly those two powerful planes that could sometimes fly at 400 miles per hour. But she would have to wait a bit, because none of the women pilots had yet flown them.

Then, in late February 1943, Nancy Love became the first woman pilot to fly the single-engine pursuit plane called the P-51 Mustang.

Evelyn and two other WAFS members would be the next to fly the P-51 in a few more months. However, it would take lots more flying before they were qualified to transport that model of plane.

It would be a while longer before Evelyn and others could even try to fly a P-38.

In the meantime, something happened that led people to wonder if women should ever be military pilots—or if they should be grounded from duty.

Chapter 26

Grounded

Evelyn's friend Cornelia Fort was an excellent pilot. Even so, she became the first WAFS pilot killed in a plane crash during the war. She died in March 1943 while flying on a ferrying mission with other men and women pilots in Army Air Force planes.

A young male pilot in that group accidentally flew his plane too close to hers. He clipped off part of her plane's wing.

His aircraft was not badly damaged, so he was able to keep flying. But with its wing broken, Cornelia's airplane went into a spin and crashed into the ground. The Army ruled her death an accident, and not her fault.

Evelyn did not see the crash, but she wrote home about it. She was troubled by her friend's death, but she and all the women pilots understood that flying was dangerous.

Cornelia's death served as a reminder that they were doing dangerous work that not everyone could do—and that an accident could happen to any one of them, in a split second, anywhere, and at any time.

Evelyn intended to keep on flying. It was her life's work, and she lived to fly. It was something she wanted to do for the rest of her life. So did most of the other women pilots.

Although the military said Cornelia's death was not her own fault, the Army was still not sure that women should be flying. The government decided to ground the women pilots and to hold talks to decide what to do with them.

Back in the Air

A few weeks later, the military issued new

orders. The women pilots could fly again. Those who could pass another test would be allowed to fly the bigger or faster war planes.

Before long, a few more of the 25 Originals proved they could fly pursuit planes, but few of them would qualify in the P-51 and P-38 models.

The first four WAFS to qualify to fly the P-51(left to right), Evelyn Sharp (on wing), Barbara Towne (above), Nancy Love (in cockpit), and Barbara Erickson (at right) (Photo Courtesy, National Museum of the U.S. Air Force)

In June, Evelyn Sharp reached another goal. She became one of the first female pilots to qualify to fly the P-51 Mustang. Barbara Towne and

Barbara Erickson were the other women pilots qualified to fly the P-51, along with Nancy Love.

The women pilots of the WAFS were making an excellent name for themselves. Soon their group name would be changed from WAFS to WASP.

Evelyn Sharp wearing a parachute and climbing into a P-51 Mustang. She was one of the first of the women pilots to qualify to fly one of these pursuit planes. (Photo Courtesy, The Woman's Collection, Texas Woman's University, Denton, Texas)

Chapter 27

From WAFS to WASP

The women pilots did their job so well that before long, the military decided to reorganize and rename their groups and increase their numbers.

General Henry "Hap" Arnold gave the order to combine Nancy Love's WAFS and Jacqueline Cochran's women pilots into one big new group. That happened on August 5, 1943.

That new group was called the Women Airforce Service Pilots. It was often nicknamed the WASP.

Jacqueline Cochran was in charge of all WASP pilots. Nancy Love was second in command.

More women trained and became part of that new program. Counting "The Original" WAFS and the new members, the Army Air Forces eventually graduated about 1,100 women pilots into that WASP program.

Those women pilots came from a wide range of social groups, educational levels, and backgrounds. They also included two Chinese Americans, Hazel Ying Lee and Maggie Gee, and a Native American woman, Ola Mildred Rexroat.

All the women had two things in common: They wanted to fly, and they wanted to help their country in a time of war.

WASP members were then sent to about 120 air bases across the U.S. Barbara Erickson became the WASP in charge of the Long Beach base. Evelyn Sharp was second in command.

Then in September 1943, Evelyn received a transfer to the base at Palm Springs, California. She was to be the WASP in charge there. She was truly a leader, but she would not be there long.

Palm Springs, California (Army Air Base) Evelyn Sharp (sitting, center front, holding purse) with some of the WASP members from that base (Mary Farmer Palmer Collection, Courtesy Palmer Family)

Chapter 28

Women Pilots in the Movies

Evelyn was only based at Palm Springs for a short time. Then that base was turned into a pursuit plane training base, so Evelyn returned to Long Beach.

There she had her picture taken with some Hollywood movie stars. The stars were at Long Beach to make a movie called *Ladies Courageous* about the women pilots who flew for the military.

Popular movie stars Loretta Young and Diana Barrymore both played WAFS. By that time, the real women pilots were no longer called WAFS. They were in the WASP program instead.

The movie makers did not really care what the

women fliers were called. Neither did the people who went to the movie when it came out the next year. They just liked the story.

Female Pilot of Another Kind

A movie maker named Walt Disney also focused on the women pilots, in a way. In 1943, he designed a female cartoon character with wings for a possible movie.

Her name was **Fifinella** (pronounced Fif uh nell luh or **Fifi**, for short), and she was also a character in a children's book called *Gremlins*.

Gremlins was a made-up story about tiny winged creatures called **gremlins** that lived in a warplane and caused problems for a pilot during World War II.

That book was written by an English Royal Air Force pilot named Roald Dahl. It was his first book, and only a few copies were printed in 1943.

(After the war, Dahl became famous as the author of the Willie Wonka book, *Charlie and the Chocolate Factory*, and other children's books.)

Walt Disney wanted to make Dahl's *Gremlins* book into a movie. So the Disney artists drew cartoons of the gremlins. They used those in a magazine, a coloring book, and a jigsaw puzzle. Someone even made a Fifinella doll.

Everything seemed to be leading toward a big cartoon movie about the gremlins, but Disney's company was afraid people would not go to a war movie about cartoon characters during that war. So, they just made a few gremlin cartoons instead.

Before then, the Disney artists had created several cartoon characters for use as military patches for different Army groups.

Fifinella seemed to be a natural one for the women pilots of the WASP. So Disney let the WASP program have her as their own special mascot. Near the end of the war, WASP members proudly wore a Fifinella patch on their uniforms.

In 2006 a new *Gremlins* book came out. It told about Fifinella as a cartoon, a World War II WASP patch and mascot, and almost a movie star.

Fifinella – WASP Mascot

Fifinella patch used by the Women Airforce Service Pilots or WASP program during World War II – Originally created by Walt Disney/Disney Studios for a Disney movie based on Roald Dahl's book *Gremlins*. Fifinella and the male Gremlins did not become movie stars, but sometimes they can still be seen in old cartoons. (Photo Courtesy, National Museum of the U.S. Air Force; also a patch from the author's collection)

Chapter 29

In Pursuit of Flying

Before World War II ended, WASP members tested out and flew almost every kind of plane flown by the men pilots in the Army Air Forces. The WASP even flew some of the big bombers.

Evelyn loved flying warplanes of any kind. She especially loved to fly the pursuit planes. Those small planes flew very fast. They could move and turn quickly. They even looked sporty— a bit like race cars or sports cars.

Pursuit planes became very popular and important during the war. They were also greatly needed.

They could escort and protect the slower,

heavier cargo and bomber planes. They could be used for scouting missions. They could also be used for attacks on, or short dogfights with, enemy planes.

Those pursuit planes were also some of the hardest to fly. There was only one seat for the pilot and no place for an instructor to sit.

The pilot had to be well prepared and able to fly the plane right—the very first time he or she flew it. There might not be a second chance, so those pilots had to be really skillful!

Evelyn was! She loved flying the P-51 Mustang. And she really wanted to fly the strange looking P-38 Lightning.

The P-38 was a twin-engine, twin-boom (that means two tail or split tail) plane. It was the first Army Air Force plane to have three landing gears (wheels or tires), like a tricycle.

Both the P-51 and the P-38 could fly farther on a tank of fuel than other pursuit planes. So they could protect planes on longer flights.

Special Delivery

As demand for the P-51 and P-38 increased, many more of those planes needed to be made. Then those new planes sat at the factories waiting to be taken to their assigned bases.

The Army Air Forces really needed those planes in the war. However, not just anyone could transport them. Only the most qualified pilots could fly them. Unfortunately, there just were not enough of those pilots available to get the planes where they needed to be.

Before long, the factories had no room to store them. Those planes were ready to go. They just needed the pilots to take them to the bases and ports and get them overseas—right away.

The Army Air Forces needed to do something. It sent out a call to all qualified P-51 or P-38 pilots.

It asked those pilots to come fly one of those planes to an assigned base. Then everyone waited for the weather to cooperate.

On December 13, 1943, everything finally cooperated. Two hundred qualified pilots showed up to fly those planes to the assigned bases.

Only two of those 200 pilots were women. One was Barbara Erickson, the WASP commander at Long Beach. The other was Evelyn Sharp. Both of those ladies flew P-51s that day.

Top Goals

In January 1944, Evelyn began working on other goals. By then, she had a grand total of 3,500 flying hours. In March of that year, she began to qualify in the B-17 Flying Fortress.

That bomber generally weighed somewhere between 32,000 to 55,000 pounds, depending upon its cargo. Evelyn weighed only 115 pounds.

People still wondered if women were strong enough to fly such heavy planes, but many female pilots had no trouble doing just that.

Evelyn had only a few more flights to make in the B-17 model to qualify to transport that plane. If she could do that, she would earn the "**Fifth**

Rating" in her pilot level or ranking. That was the highest possible rating for pilots in the ferrying groups.

It was also the highest rating a woman pilot could achieve at that time. Evelyn set her next goal. She wanted to qualify in the B-17 and pass that Fifth Rating as soon as she could.

But before she could qualify in the B-17, she received orders to ferry several other planes. One of those was a B-26 Marauder bomber. The B-26 was made by the Martin Aviation Company of Omaha, in her home state of Nebraska.

A Very Dangerous Plane To Fly

Around then, Evelyn also began training in her favorite kind of pursuit plane. That was the speedy, sporty P-38 Lightning that pilots either loved or hated. With its two engines and twin tail (or split tail), it could be a hard plane to fly—and a very dangerous one.

Having two engines was a good thing for the P-38. Those two engines gave the plane great speed and long range. However, the engines on the P-38 also had a bad reputation. Sometimes they just quit working while in the air.

In some cases, if one engine quit (especially the left one, at a low **altitude**), the P-38 would spin itself into the ground. Even experienced men pilots had lost their lives at the controls of that plane.

The P-38 Lightning, a sporty pursuit plane with twin engines, a twin tail, and a bad reputation for crashes - Evelyn's favorite plane (Photo Courtesy, National Museum of the U.S. Air Force)

The company that developed the P-38 had made engine changes and other changes during the few years the plane was in production.

More changes would come. But the plane still had a bad reputation. It could be a very dangerous plane to fly, especially at takeoff.

The P-38 was a great pursuit or escort plane, as long as it was working fine and if it had a good pilot. Evelyn was a great pilot, but she was also new to that kind of plane. She had just qualified to fly it in late March 1944. She would soon try to ferry one across country.

Evelyn Sharp's Last Flight
From Long Beach, California, to Newark, New Jersey

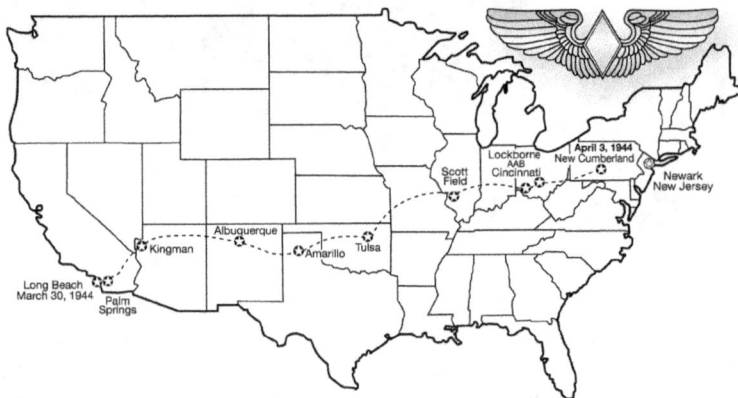

Evelyn's last flight was to ferry a brand new P-38 from Long Beach, California (far left), across country to Newark, New Jersey, on a scheduled five-day journey from March 30 to April 3, 1944 (map by Ronald E. Lukesh)

Chapter 30

Evelyn's Last Flight

In the last week of March, 1944, Evelyn received orders to ferry a P-38 Lightning pursuit plane. She was to take the plane from Long Beach, California, to Newark, New Jersey.

The first four days of that five-day journey took her from Long Beach to Palm Springs, California, then over Arizona to New Mexico, and on over Texas and Oklahoma. From there she flew on to Illinois, Ohio, and Pennsylvania.

The final leg, or the last day of flying for that journey, should have taken her from Pennsylvania to Newark, New Jersey, where the plane would be loaded on a ship and taken overseas. But things would not go as planned.

Evelyn began that journey on March 30. She stopped at bases or airfields all along the way. At each one, she had her plane refueled. She also had her airplane engines checked. She needed to be sure they always had the right amount of oil and the right oil pressure.

At each stop, she made notes in her logbook about such details. At night, she stayed over at one of the bases or at a hotel.

On the fourth day of that trip, she flew north into Ohio and Pennsylvania. She headed for the city of Harrisburg. Before she could get there, a late snowstorm with sleet and rain made flying difficult.

Women transport pilots were not allowed to fly in bad weather, even if they had an instrument rating, like Evelyn did. So Evelyn had to find an airfield and land.

She landed at the nearby New Cumberland Airport near Beacon Hill shortly after noon on

April 2. The weather and the WASP rules would not let her continue flying that day.

Staying in Touch

After landing, Evelyn made notes in her logbook. She also found a hotel room for the night.

She spent the rest of the day writing letters to her friends, her family, and her many fans. She always liked to keep in touch with people all over the country.

That day, she even wrote to her birth father, Orla Crouse. For her next mission, she was scheduled to deliver a plane to Montana. There she and her father planned to meet—for the very first time. Sadly, that meeting would never happen.

On the morning of April 3, 1944, Evelyn mailed some of her letters. She had others she planned to finish later. She put those in her purse.

Then she ran into one or two men pilots she knew and had breakfast at the airport with them. One of those men later reported that Evelyn told him she had been having some trouble with one of her P-38 engines all across the country.

Ready to Fly

After breakfast, Evelyn went to her plane. She checked all around the outside of the silver P-38 Lightning.

When everything looked okay to her, she climbed into the pilot's seat. She pre-checked everything there and then started the engines.

The plane looked and sounded fine. Everything seemed to be all ready to go for the last leg of her journey—just one more short flight, from the Harrisburg area to New Jersey.

After that, she planned to work on her next goals:

- to meet her real father for the first time,
- to qualify in the B-17,
- and to earn her Fifth Rating—the highest rating allowed for women pilots.

But none of those things would happen.

Chapter 31

Gone in Less Than a Minute

Everything appeared to be fine. So Evelyn Sharp taxied the sporty P-38 down the runway that morning of April 3, 1944.

She was heading for Newark and then on to her next mission. She was doing what she loved most—flying—in her favorite kind of plane. What could be better? And what could go wrong?

The wind blew from the wrong direction that day, so she had to take off uphill. But that did not seem to be a problem at the time.

She revved up her engines, took her feet off the brakes, and tore off into the sky at 10:29 A.M.

Just a few seconds later, she knew she was in

trouble—life-threatening trouble!

She was only 700 feet above the ground. Then with no warning, her left engine just quit! A puff of smoke rose up into the sky.

For only an instant, the plane hung in the air. Then it dropped sharply as it tried to twist itself into the ground.

Immediately Evelyn reacted. She used all her strength and skill to keep the aircraft level.

She was able to straighten the plane and keep it right side up, but the loss of one engine dropped the aircraft like a brick.

She was too close to the ground and coming down fast. Her parachute would not help her.

In the few seconds she had left, she looked for a place to land—but she could not find a good place!

To her right, she saw the many houses of Harrisburg. To the left she saw Beacon Hill with its radio towers on top—and lots of trees.

But there were acres of farmland nearby, too.

She headed for the only place where she might possibly land—the farmland and a hill that seemed to be rising up to meet her.

She had landed on farm fields before, perhaps she could do it again—if she could just stay away from the radio towers and the trees.

Unfortunately, she was running out of everything—altitude, landing room, and time!

Suddenly, one P-38 wingtip snagged on some tree branches and pulled the plane that way—toward a hill.

She regained control and steered for the hill. There was nowhere else for her to go.

As slowly as she could, she brought the plane down—almost straight down—in what was called a pancake landing.

She almost made it, but the plane came down too hard and too fast.

The P-38 crashed onto the hill, hard, on its belly. It skidded about ten feet forward. Then it came to a stop.

The Crash

People at the airport watched in horror.

In the kitchen of their nearby farmhouse, a farmer and his wife heard one of the plane's engines stop. Soon they heard a thud. The farmer ran to the crash site as fast as he could.

As the airplane hit the ground, the landing wheels pushed up through the underside of the plane.

Instantly the seat broke loose. It shot upward, sending the young pilot's body up against the window-like **canopy**—and out.

Both she and the canopy landed on the ground about eight feet ahead and to the right of the plane.

Some smoke drifted up from the left engine.

Fearing the plane would catch fire and explode, the farmer ran up and tried to save the pilot. As carefully as possible, he picked her up and carried her away from the crash.

Gently, he put her body down a safe distance from the plane. Then he waved his arms in the air as a small plane flew over the crash site. It was flown by the airport safety director.

Too Late

By then it was already too late for the P-38 pilot. WASP Evelyn Sharp, age 24, had died instantly—of a broken neck—when the plane first hit the ground. It happened so fast that she probably felt no pain.

All that had happened in less than a minute. The clock in the P-38 had stopped at the exact moment of the crash. It read 10:30 a.m.

Strangely, one of the letters she had mailed to Ord that morning was marked with that same time and date. Other letters found in her purse at the crash site would be mailed later by family and friends.

Evelyn had done all she could to try to save herself and the plane. The loss of that engine at that low level had just caused the plane to come down too hard and too fast.

If she had just been higher in the sky when the

engine quit—or if the runway had been longer or downhill—then she might have been able to land the plane safely instead.

None of that mattered. Evelyn Sharp's short but remarkable life was over.

The WASP program would outlive her by only eight months.

The broken P-38 at the crash site where Evelyn died. Note the military man checking out the scene. (Mary Farmer Palmer Collection, Courtesy Palmer Family)

Chapter 32

Coming Home

When Jacqueline Cochran received word of the crash, she sent Evelyn's mother this telegram:

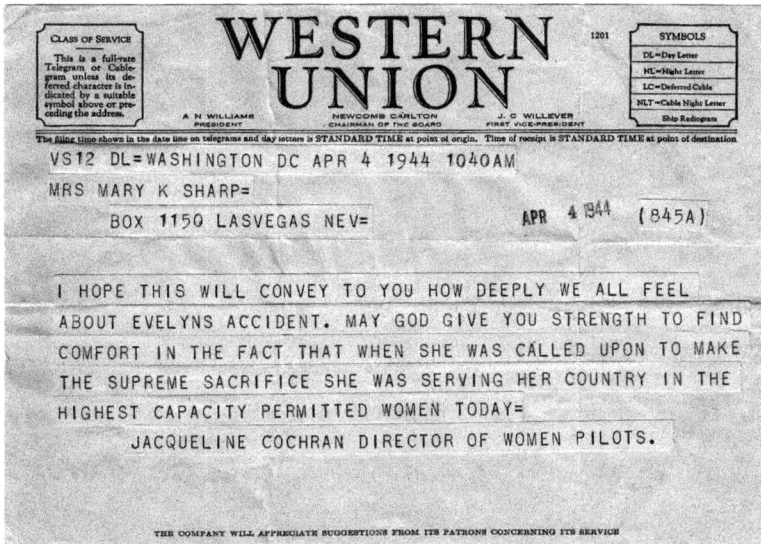

(Mary Farmer Palmer Collection, Courtesy of Palmer Family)

Nancy Love and the rest of the WASP members could not believe the news about Evelyn's crash.

Evelyn was one of their best pilots. She had one of the highest ratings. She often had the most flight hours and experience of all of them. They all liked her. Her death made no sense to anyone.

The crash was another reminder that they were doing a very dangerous job, and not something everyone could do—but a job they all loved.

To make things worse, the WASP fliers were not really a part of the military. It did not matter that they flew for the Army Air Forces. As a WASP, Evelyn had no insurance. Her family would receive no money to pay for her funeral.

As the WASP members had done before, for Evelyn's friend Cornelia and for others, they took up a collection. They raised $200 to send home to Evelyn's family to help pay for her funeral.

Fellow WASP member Nancy Batson had

known Evelyn in both the WAFS and WASP programs. Nancy Love ordered Batson to ride in the train that would take Evelyn's body home to Ord, and to stay there for the funeral.

Hometown Hero

In Ord, Nancy Batson met John and Mary Sharp and Elsie Crouse Rick—Evelyn's adopted parents and her birth mother. Batson also met the people of Ord who came to honor their hometown hero.

Evelyn Sharp was buried in the Ord Cemetery on Easter Sunday, April 9, 1944. Hundreds of people came to say their goodbyes. Ord's favorite daughter had come home for the very last time.

Evelyn's friend Nancy Batson was there in a WASP uniform. She represented the whole Women Airforce Service Pilot group at the funeral.

Batson did her most respectful best. She did it well. She stood at attention and did not shed a tear for her friend—until later when she was alone. That helped others at the funeral stay strong, too.

WASP members were not supposed to be buried with military honors. Still, an old man at Evelyn's funeral asked if he could drape an American flag over her coffin.

Nancy Batson thought about the question for a moment. Congress was discussing that issue just that week. What would it hurt? Nancy Batson smiled and said softly, "Of course you can." Someone else played *Taps* at the gravesite.

No one saw anything wrong with any of that. Evelyn had done her part and more for the military and for her country.

To the people who knew her and to others who had heard of her, Evelyn was a hero. To them, she was as much a military hero as the men she had taught to fly in the war. She had even been flying a military plane on its way to war.

Not long after the funeral, a simple white cross and a stone monument were put in place to mark Evelyn Sharp's gravesite there. Many years later, a plaque was added.

Evelyn Sharp's grave markers in the Ord Cemetery - The graves of John and Mary Sharp (Evelyn's adopted parents) are to the left and right of her markers. (Photo by Ron Lukesh, 2011)

Reasons to Remember

Nancy Batson would remember Evelyn Sharp and that funeral for the rest of her life. She had good reason to remember her friend and that P-38 crash.

Oddly enough, just eight months after

Evelyn's funeral, Nancy Batson almost crashed in a P-38, too. Like Evelyn, she was on the final leg of a ferrying mission to Newark. There her plane had both a landing gear problem and an engine problem.

For two hours, Nancy tried to land her crippled plane. She said later that just thinking about Evelyn's accident helped her remain calm and helped her finally land that plane safely.

Two other Original WAFS and WASP members had scary problems with P-38s, too. One of those was Barbara Erickson who often called Evelyn her best friend.

The other was Betty Gillies. She almost crashed at the same airfield where Evelyn died. Betty's P-38 also had engine trouble, but the wind was right for her that day. So Betty was taking off downhill. Because of that, she was high enough to go around and land safely.

For the rest of their lives, those WASP members and others remembered their time in the air. They also remembered the loss of their friend and fellow pilot, Evelyn Sharp—a pilot they had known, admired, learned from, and often looked up to.

Others would remember Evelyn and the members of the WASP, as well.

Chapter 33

In Honor of Evelyn and the WASP

On December 20, 1944, the Army ended its Women Airforce Service Pilots program. That happened about eight months after Evelyn's accident and about eight months before the end of World War II.

General Hap Arnold had given the order to start the WASP program. He also gave the order to end it.

A few weeks before that, he gave a speech at Avenger Field in Texas. That was the training base and official home base of the WASP.

There General Arnold said, "The WASP have completed their mission. Their job has been successful. But as is usual in war, the cost has been heavy. Thirty-eight WASP have died while helping their country move toward the moments of final victory. The Air Forces will long remember their service and their final **sacrifice**."

One of the 38 WASP had been Evelyn Sharp.

On that same day, another military man, General Barton Yount, also gave a speech. He, too, talked about the 38 WASP members who died in service. He said, "Let us pay tribute to these women by honoring their memory....Let us treasure their memory as women whose sacrifice has brought honor not only to their country, but also to their organization."

He added, "We shall not forget the accomplishments of our women fliers and their contributions to the fulfillment of our mission."

Hometown Honors

The people of Ord and of Nebraska still honor Evelyn's accomplishments. They are very proud of their best known woman pilot and of her **legacy**.

Evelyn Sharp Field Dedication at Ord, Nebraska, 1948 (Photo Courtesy of Diane Ruth Armour Bartels)

In 1948, just a few years after Evelyn's funeral, Ord Air Field was renamed Evelyn Sharp Field. The small building there is a monument and a small museum to her memory. Photos and news clippings decorate the walls and counters. The road nearby was also renamed for her.

Two airplane propellers now stand guard at that airfield. One is from a Curtiss Robin airplane Evelyn once owned. The other is from a P-38.

In 1996, the town of Ord held its first Evelyn Sharp Day at the airport. Nancy Batson, who had been in Ord for Evelyn's funeral, flew back for that celebration.

So did author and pilot Diane Ruth Armour Bartels, who had just written a book about Evelyn.

Evelyn Sharp Day is now held in Ord almost every year. There and then, Evelyn's memory and story are celebrated.

Honored By Her State

Evelyn has also been honored by her state. In 1992, her name was added individually to the Nebraska Aviation Hall of Fame. Then, in 2010, her name was added to that Hall of Fame again as part of the group of 19 Nebraska WASP members from World War II.

A 2010 monument to the WASP of World

War II now stands in the **Veterans** Memorial Garden at Antelope Park in Lincoln, too. That monument lists Evelyn and all 19 of the Nebraska WASP members from that war. A brick inscribed with Evelyn's name and the words "WAFS/WASP Pilot" is displayed on the World War II brick wall in that same park.

The United States Remembers the WASP

The United States also remembers Evelyn and the WASP program.

The WASP members of World War II had flown for the military but had never officially been a part of the military. So they did not receive military benefits for their years of service during World War II—not until 1977. Then, in that year, Congress granted official military status to former WASP members.

After all those years, the women of the WASP could finally receive medical benefits, be buried in the nation's military cemeteries, and have American flags on their coffins at funerals.

In 1994, a monument to the WASP was also placed in Memorial Park at the National Museum of the United States Air Force, at Wright-Patterson Air Force Base in Ohio.

Then, in 2010—about 65 years after the end of World War II—the WASP received a very special award. At that time, surviving members of the Women Airforce Service Pilots (or their families) received Congressional Gold Medals at a ceremony in Washington, D.C.

Those medals are the highest honor any civilian can receive for service to our country, the United States of America.

Congressional Gold Medal for the WASP Veterans – Original medal from the collection of *Sharpie* author Diane Ruth Armour Bartels. Copy of the medal, front and back, from the *Sky Rider* author's collection (Photos by Ron Lukesh)

Nebraska pilot Diane Bartels was there. She had written the book *Sharpie! The Life Story of Evelyn Sharp, Nebraska's Aviatrix* in 1996. She received one of the special WASP gold medals in Evelyn's honor at that ceremony.

That award honoring Evelyn and the other WASP members was long overdue.

Chapter 34

Lofty Goals

A few months before World War II started, a reporter asked Evelyn Sharp if she would volunteer for service if America went to war. She replied that she would do whatever she could to help. And she did!

Evelyn Sharp did not live very long—just a few months more than 24 years. She never married or had children. But she left a legacy of courage, honor, leadership, and **mentorship** that still stands today. She was a hero and role model.

She was a leader in the women's movement for **equality**, too—just as Amelia Earhart, Nancy Love, Jackie Cochran, and others were. Evelyn believed in something that Amelia Earhart once said many years before: "Women must try to do things as men have tried. When they fail, their failure must be but a challenge to others."

Evelyn often set goals for herself during her short life. She achieved many of those.

Other women who followed took up the challenge and achieved more. As another WASP once said, "You can be whatever you set your heart and head to be, and don't let anybody tell you you can't be, because [about 1,100] women pilots did it in World War II."

The women of the WASP flew because they loved flying and loved the job they did. They did that job well, with few thoughts of glory. They did their best to help their country—and to enjoy their short time in the sky.

Evelyn loved being a sky rider. Who knows what greater heights she might have reached if she had been in a different plane or on a different runway that April day in 1944.

The sky was the limit for her—and it still is, for others. In fact, many of today's women pilots and astronauts often credit the World War II WASP as the inspiration for their own successes.

Evelyn was one of those great ones who led the way—one of the first female pilots trained to fly for the military—and she was truly a role model to look up to and to remember.

Nancy Love, Evelyn's friend and former commander, died in 1976. Among her things was found a handwritten list of the 38 WASP who died during World War II. Love kept that list to honor and remember those pilots she had known and respected, women who had flown bravely and given their lives for their country—including Evelyn Sharp—one of Love's 25 "Originals."

This is the story of Evelyn Sharp, a little girl who made a wish to drive an airplane, and of the woman pilot she became, a pilot who set high-flying goals, overcame many problems, and reached great heights in times of war and peace.

Critical Thinking Questions:

About Evelyn Sharp

1. Make a list of positive character traits that describe Evelyn. Choose one that you think best describes her and tell why you chose that one. Compare with someone else's choice.
2. Why do you think Evelyn and her family moved so often?
3. What did Evelyn do for fun, or for her family, or for her community?
4. What are some of the problems Evelyn faced as a child, as a teenager, or as an adult?
5. Why do you think the people of the 1920s and 1930s were so interested in planes and flying?
6. What kinds of things did barnstormers do to try to get people to come to air shows and air rodeos, and why?
7. How important was goal setting in Evelyn's life? How did that help her become successful?
8. Why was it important for Evelyn to treat flying as a business and to belong to the right kinds of groups?
9. How and why did Dr. Glen Auble and the people of Ord try to help Evelyn?
10. Why did the government want to start the Civilian Pilot Training Program (CPTP)?
11. Why do you think Evelyn did not accept Jackie Cochran's invitation to fly in Europe?

12. Why do you think Evelyn accepted Nancy Love's invitation to transport planes (WAFS)?
13. Who or what were "The Originals"?
14. Why did Evelyn like flying for the military?
15. How did the military treat the women pilots?
16. Before World War II, many women stayed home and did not work outside of the house. How and why do you think that changed in the 1940s?
17. Why did people call Evelyn such names as "Sharpie," "Sky Rider," and the "Best of the Best"?
18. Use resources to find the names of WASP members from your home state. Which of them were "originals"? Which of them were in other women pilot groups?
19. How does your community, state, or nation honor people who served in the military?
20. If Evelyn Sharp had not died in that P-38 plane crash, what do you think she would have done with the rest of her life, and why?
21. Use resources to find out how women helped our country in World War II or other wars.
22. What do you think happened to some of the women pilots after the WASP were disbanded.
23. In what ways did Evelyn and the other WASP members set the standard and pave the way for today's women pilots or women in the military?

Bibliographies

Nonfiction Sources:

Abernathy, Irene (Auble). *My Friend, Evelyn Sharp.* Voices From the Past. Hall County [NE] Historical Society [Presentation]. Grand Island, NE: February 13, 2011.

Aircraft: World Wars I & II. Stamford, CT: Longmeadow Press, 1988.

Auble, Glen. *The story of Evelyn Sharp's Aeroplane Experience.* [Unpublished paper], n.d.

Bartels, Diane Ruth Armour. *Sharpie! The Life Story of Evelyn Sharp, Nebraska's Aviatrix.* Lincoln, NE: Dageforde Publishing, 1996.

Boyne, Walter J. *The Smithsonian Book of Flight.* Washington, DC: Smithsonian Institute, 1987.

Caidin, Martin. *Fork-Tailed Devil: The P-38.* Bantam Air & Space series. New York: Bantam, 1971, 1973.

Carl, Ann B. *A WASP Among Eagles: A Woman Military Test Pilot in World War II.* Washington DC: Smithsonian Institute Press, 1999.

Churchill, Jan. *On Wings to War: Teresa James, Aviator.* Manhattan, KS: Sunflower University Press, 1992.

Dahl, Roald. *The Gremlins: A Royal Air Force Story: The Lost Walt Disney Production.* Walt Disney Productions, 1943. Reprinted Milwaukee, OR: Dark Horse Books, 2006.

Davis, Larry. *P-38 Lightning in Action.* Aircraft Number 109. Carrollton, TX: Squadron/Signal Publications, 1990.

Dill, Graydon. "The End of the Runway." *Nebraskaland Magazine.* March 1988, pp. 32-45.

Fly Girls. [Documentary VHS]. The American Experience series. Boston, MA: PBS, WGBH, 1999.

Grand Island Independent. Various articles/issues.

Keil, Sally Van Wagenen. *Those Wonderful Women in Their Flying Machines: The Unknown Heroines of World War II.* New York: Four Directions Press, 1979, 1990.

Kral, E.A. *Evelyn Sharp. http:*www.nsea.org/news/SharpProfile.htm

Lukesh, Jean A. *Evelyn Sharp.* [Unpublished paper]. 1990.

National Museum of the U.S. Air Force. www.nationalmuseum.af.mil/

Nebraska Aviation Hall of Fame. www.aero.state.ne.us/hofmenu.htm

Noggle, Anne. *For God, Country, and the Thrill of It: Women Airforce Service Pilots in World War II.* College Station, Texas A&M University Press, 1990.

Ord Quiz newspaper. Various articles/issues.

Palmer Family. [Communications, photos, and more], 2011.

Rickman, Sarah Byrn. *Nancy Batson Crews: Alabama's First Lady of Flight.* Tuscaloosa, AL: University of Alabama Press, 2009.

Rickman, Sarah Byrn. *Nancy Love and the WASP Ferry Pilots of*

World War II. Denton, TX: University of North Texas Press, 2008.

Rickman, Sarah Byrn. *The Originals: The Women's Auxiliary Ferrying Squadron of World War II*. Sarasota, FL: Disc-Us Books, 2001.

Sharpie—Born to Fly. [Documentary DVD]. Linoln, NE: NET [Nebraska Educational Television], 2000.

Simbeck, Rob. *Daughter of the Air: The Brief Soaring Life of Cornelia Fort*. New York: Atlantic Monthly Press, 1999.

Smithsonian's National Air and Space Museum. www.nasm.si.edu

Verges, Marianne. *On Silver Wings: The Women Airforce Service Pilots of World War II, 1942-1944*. New York: Ballantine, 1991.

WASP Museum. [Website]. http:waspmuseum.org

WASP on the Web or Wings Across America website. www.wingacrossamerica.us/wasp/

Williams, Vera S. *WASPs: Women Airforce Service Pilots of World War II*. Osceola, WI: Motorbooks International, 1994.

Woman Airforce Service Pilots. Texas Woman's University. Denton, Texas. www.twu.edu

"Women: Here Come the WAFS." *Time Magazine*, June 7, 1943. p.60.

Zeinert, Karen. *Those Incredible Women of World War II*. Brookfield, CT: Millbrook, 1994.

Educator Resources:
1925-1949: The War: Nebraska Stories [Lesson Plans]. www.nebraskastudies.org/0800/resources/09stories.pdf

Centennial of Flight. http://www.centennialofflight.gov/index.cfm

Lukesh, Jean A. *Nebraska Adventure*. [Textbook]. Layton, Utah: Gibbs Smith Co., 2004/2005.

Nebraska Trailblazers #18 Aviation in Nebraska and #21 Nebraskans in World War II. Nebraska State Historical Society. www.nebraskahistory.org/museum/teachers/material/trailist.htm

Wasp Museum. [Website] http://waspmuseum.org/education/

WASP on the Web or *Wings Across America* website. http://www.wingacrossamerica.us/wasp

Related Children's and YA Nonfiction Books/Materials
Atkins, Jeannine. *Wings and Rockets: The Story of Women in Air and Space*. Farrar, Straus & Giroux, 2003. (gr 5-10, YA)

Colman, Penny. *Rosie the Riveter; Women Working on the Home Front in World War II*. Crown, 1998. (gr 6-9).

Gorley, Beatrice. *Amelia Earhart: Young Aviator*. Childhood of Famous Americans series. Aladdin, 2000. (ages 9-12).

Gourley, Catherine, et. al. *Welcome to Molly's World: 1944: Growing Up in World War II America*. American Girls Collection. American Girl, October 1999. (ages 8 & up).

Jerome, Kate Boehm. *Who Was Amelia Earhart?* Grosset & Dunlap, 2002. (ages 9-12)

Krull, Kathleen. *V Is for Victory: America Remembers World War II.* American History Classics. Knopf, 2002. (gr 7 & up)

Langley, Wanda. *Flying Higher: The Women Airforce Service Pilots of World War II.* Linnet Books, 2002. (YA)

May, Elaine Tyler. *Pushing the Limits: American Women, 1940-1961.* Oxford University Press, 1998. (ages 12 & up, YA)

Molly – *An American Girl on the Home Front.* [DVD] American Girls Collection. American Girl, 2006.

Moss, Marissa. *Sky High: The True Story of Maggie Gee.* Tricycle Press, 2009. (grades 1-4).

Nathan, Amy. *Yankee Doodle Gals: Women Pilots of World War II.* National Geographic, 2001. (ages 8 & up).

Smith, Elizabeth S. *Coming Out Right: The Story of Jackie Cochran.* Walker, 1991. (grades 5-8)

Stone, Tanya Lee. *Amelia Earhart.* Dorling Kindersley, 2007. (ages 9-12).

Whitman, Sylvia. *Uncle Sam Wants You! Military Men and Women of World War II.* Lerner, 1993. (gr 7+).

Related Children's and YA Fiction Books:

Hart, Alison. *A Spy on the Home Front: A Molly Mystery.* American Girls series. American Girl, 2005. (ages 8 & up)

Smith, Sherri. *Flygirl.* Putnam, 2009. (YA)

Tripp, Valerie. *Molly Takes Flight.* American Girls series. American Girl, 1999. (ages 7 *& up) (also Molly Doll and WASP Outfit)

Zeinert, Karen. *To Touch the Stars: A Story of World War II.* Jamestown's American Portraits series. Brighter Child, 2004. (gr. 5-8)

Glossary:

99s: See Ninety-Nines.

aerobatics: a very skillful kind of advanced flying

Aeronca C-3: a kind of small plane

aeroplane: the old spelling for airplane or plane

Air Transport Command (ATC): the name for the large group of men and women pilots who ferried military planes in WWII. The WAFS and WASP were experimental groups within the ATC program.

altitude: how high above ground or sea level something is

ammunition: bullets

Army Air Forces: a branch of the military that was originally a part of the Army and was first known as the Army Air Corps until six months before the start of World War II when it became the Army Air Forces or AAF. In 1947, after the end of World War II, the AAF became a separate branch of the military known as the U.S. Air Force.

artillery: large or heavy duty military guns

asthma: a condition that causes breathing problems

ATC: See Air Transport Command

athlete: someone who is good at sports

athletic: good at sports

auxiliary: additional, extra, or special

aviation: flying airplanes

barnstormers: early day pilots who flew very low to the ground

barracks: buildings used as bedrooms for many soldiers

boarding house: a house where people can rent a room for a long time, like a hotel or bed-and-breakfast with longer stays

cabinet: some of the highest members of the American government

canopy: the glass-like covering over the pilot of a warplane

cargo planes: big planes that can carry lots of men and heavy cargo, such as materials, equipment, and other vehicles

chapter: a local club or group that is associated with a national organization or group

civilian: someone who is not in the military

Civilian Pilot Training Program: a program to teach people to fly planes so they could join the military as pilots

cockpit: the area of a plane where the pilot sits

CPTP: abbreviation for Civilian Pilot Training Program

combat: fighting, war, or battle

commercial: for business or profit; a **transport license** is also called a **commercial license**

Curtiss Robin: a kind of small plane

Dirty Thirties: Nickname for the 1930s when the weather was very dry and windy. See also **Great Depression**.

equality: being treated as an equal and respected person

ferry: to transport or take something from one place to another, as to fly a plane from the company that made it to an air base

Fifinella (fif uh nell luh): female gremlin created by Roald Dahl and Walt Disney; mascot of the WASP group

Fifi: nickname for Fifinella

Fifth Rating: the highest rating possible for women pilots

Flyabout: the name of a small plane

flying circuses: another name for air shows

Great Depression: Time period for 1929 through the 1930s, after the stock market crashed and many people lost everything they owned. See also **Dirty Thirties**.

gremlin: imaginary character that plays tricks on people

grounded: not allowed to fly

hangar: a building where airplanes are kept at an airport

instrument rating: a license that says a pilot is qualified to use special flight instruments to fly in bad weather when visibility is a problem

jodhpurs: wide-hipped pants often worn by early pilots, military men, and horseback riders

legacy: something of value in history or handed down to the next generation

logbook: a pilot's official record book of all flying activities

mentor: role model, teacher, or special friend who teaches good, positive life lessons

mentorship: quality of being a good role model

mess hall: Army lunchroom

navigator: a person who uses maps to see how to get from one place to another

navigation: knowing how to use maps and instruments to get from one place to another

Ninety-Nines (or 99s): a national group of women pilots, named for the 99 women who accepted Amelia Earhart's invitation to join her aviation club

Originals: the name for the first group of 25 WAFS

orphanage: a place that takes in orphans or children who have no parents

parachute: lightweight fabric attached to a person or to something to make it float down from the sky slowly

passenger: a person who goes for a ride

polka: a kind of music often played at dances

polio: a crippling disease of the early 1900s.

propeller: a set of turning blades at the front of a plane that help the plane move forward

pursuit planes: small fast military planes, often used to chase away enemy planes or to protect other planes

qualifications: achievements needed to join a group or do something

qualify: meet certain restrictions

rickets: a weakening of the bones, caused by a lack of vitamins and minerals

sacrifice: to give up something of value for a good cause

solo: fly a plane alone

squadron: a military group, often made up of pilots and crews

Stinson-Detroiter: a kind of 5- or 6-passenger small plane

Taylor Cub: a kind of small plane

telegram: early form of electronic message that uses Morse code

telegraph: the machine and wires used to send telegrams

trainee: someone just learning a job

transport: take people or things from one place to another

uniform: special clothes worn by people in the Army, Air Force, Navy, police, or other kinds of services

veterans: people who have served in the military

WAFS: see **Women's Auxiliary Ferrying Squadron**

WASP: see **Women Airforce Service Pilots**

Women Airforce Service Pilots (WASP): women trained to fly American military planes to bases or ports so men pilots could fly them in World War II

Women's Auxiliary Ferrying Squadron (WAFS or W.A.F.S.): women pilots who flew planes to men for use in World War II (WAFS later became the WASP)

Index

About the Author
Dr. Jean A. Lukesh

(M.A.Ed., History; M.A.Ed. English;
Ed.D., Curriculum & Instruction;
Graduate, Denver University Publishing Institute)

Jean Lukesh worked for thirty years as a public school Librarian, Media Specialist, Integration Specialist, Technology Representative, and classroom Teacher. She is probably best known for her popular Reluctant Reader booktalks and American History books. Now retired from everyday teaching, she writes, edits, and publishes books for children and adults, gives history and writing presentations and workshops, and mentors other authors.

Her award-winning *Nebraska Adventure*, a 4th grade Nebraska Studies textbook (©2004, 2005), is very popular with children, teachers, and other adults of all ages. Awards for that book include the 2005 national Texty Award for Excellence in El-Hi Humanities/Social Sciences, the 2006 Nebraska Center for the Book Award, and the 2006 Moonshell Arts and Humanities Council's Children's Nonfiction Award.

Working with fellow Nebraskan Ben Kuroki, Dr. Lukesh then wrote *Lucky Ears: The True Story of Ben Kuroki, World War II Hero* (©2010). That is the first book in her Noteworthy Americans series of Quick Reader biographies for kids 10 to 110. In 2011, *Lucky Ears* received a national/international Bronze Medal IPPY Book Award for Multicultural Nonfiction for Children/Teens/Young Adults and a national/international Bronze Medal Moonbeam Children's Book Award for Multicultural Nonfiction for Young Adults.

Dr. Lukesh has received many other honors and awards including the Nebraska Library Association's 2010 Mari Sandoz Award.

Sky Rider:
The Story of Evelyn Sharp, World War II WASP

In the 1920s, a little girl in Nebraska looked up and said, "Daddy, someday I want to drive an airplane." From that moment on, Evelyn Sharp set her course to become one of America's youngest and best pilots.

Overcoming adoption, asthma, and hard times, she set goals that led her to fly her own plane as a teenager and to teach men to fly for the coming war.

As one of the first members of the WASP, or Women Airforce Service Pilots, she flew all kinds of warplanes across America so that men could take them into combat in World War II. Although killed in a plane crash, Evelyn Sharp served as a great and inspiring role model for the women pilots of her day—and her legacy continues to inspire the pilots of today and tomorrow.

Sky Rider (©2011), the third book in the Noteworthy Americans series of Quick Reader biographies. Suggested for young adults, ages 11 to 112. ****

Wolves in Blue: Stories of the North Brothers and Their Pawnee Scouts (©2011) who protected travelers, settlers, and transcontinental railroad workers along the overland trails of Nebraska and across the Great Plains during the Plains Indian Wars of the 1860s and 1870s. This is the second book in the Noteworthy Americans series of Quick Reader biographies. Suggested for ages 11 to 112.

Lucky Ears: The True Story of Ben Kuroki, World War II Hero (©2010) was the first book in the Noteworthy Americans series of Quick Reader biographies and won a 2011 national/international Bronze Medal IPPY Book Award for Multicultural Nonfiction for Children/Teens/ Young Adults and a 2011 national/international Bronze Medal IPPY Book Award for Multicultural Nonfiction for Young Adults. For ages 10 to 112.

Go to: **www.fieldmousebooks.com**
to see new books in progress as part of the
NOTEWORTHY AMERICANS
Biography SERIES

Quick Order Information

More Books may be ordered on line at:
amazon.com
barnesandnoble.com

School Orders in Quantity may be made at
fieldmousebooks.com or at
jeanlukesh@aol.com Subject line: **Quantity Books**

For Author Book Talks: e-mail jeanlukesh@aol.com
Subject line: **Book Talks**

"We have **FREE Downloadable Book Covers** and
Award Symbols in Color for Bulletin Board Use."
jeanlukesh@aol.com Subject line: **Covers**

Field Mouse
BOOKS

PO Box 392 - Grand Island NE - 68802-0392

www.ingramcontent.com/pod-product-compliance
Lightning Source LLC
LaVergne TN
LVHW051523080426
835509LV00017B/2178